Understanding and Interpersor

Well-being of Married Couples. The Role of Compassion and Forgiveness

MW01515906

PRIYANKA PARIHAR

CONTENTS

CHAPTER - 1
INTRODUCTION

INTRODUCTION

Robert Quillen has observed that a happy marriage is the union of two forgivers. Forgiveness has been assumed to play an important role in human relationships of all sorts but its systematic empirical inquiry took a new momentum only after the establishment of Positive Psychology in 2000. The effectiveness of forgiveness in clinical and counselling practices has been evinced in many studies which reported that mental and physical health is significantly shaped by forgiveness (Harris & Thoresen, 2005). Giving and receiving forgiveness is significant for a romantic relationship, marital longevity and satisfaction (Fenell, 1993). It is also critical for the healing process for relationship transgressions, like infidelity (Gordon et al., 2005) and everyday relationship hurts (Fincham et al., 2004). Forgiveness requires to forget about the transgression and reconcile with the offender (Kearns & Fincham, 2004), and acceptance, condone and excuse are important for forgiveness. Recently, the construct of forgiveness has been defined in a new perspective that views it as a process of change that makes a person to become less motivated to think, feel and behave negatively pertaining to offenders (Worthington, 2005). It has been posited that forgiveness is extended as it is an altruistic gift (Worthington, 2005) or a cancellation of debt (Exline & Baumeister, 2000). Forgiveness is both intrapersonal and interpersonal that involves intra-individual and pro-social change towards a perceived transgression situated in a specific interpersonal context (McCullough et al., 2000). It involves changes that occur through an intentional process driven by a deliberate decision to forgive (McCullough et al., 2000; Worthington, 2005).

It has been argued that forgiveness is the cornerstone of a successful marriage (Worthington, 1994). Forgiveness can help couples to deal with existing difficulties, prevent the emergence of future problems (Worthington & DiBlasio, 1990) and to sustain the relationship (Mahoney et al., 2005). It has been argued that forgiveness is important when marital assumptions or relationship standards have been breached (Gordon et al., 2000), and transgressions violate partners' relational ethics and sense of justice in the marriage (Hargrave & Sells, 1997). It is also important to understand the relationship between marital satisfaction (Fincham & Linfield, 1997), couple conflict and attributions or explanations for spousal behaviour commitment in the relationship between offender and victim, and empathy experienced by the victim toward the offender (Fincham et al., 2005).

There is growing evidence that forgiveness and compassion are important predictors of happiness and well-being (Barnard & Curry, 2011; MacBeth & Gumley, 2012). It has been suggested that the realization of one's offence may lead to poor well-being. Forgiveness and compassion are characterized by pro-social and adaptive behaviours which are linked to a variety of positive life outcomes (Neff et al., 2005; Witvliet, 2005). These psychological constructs are also closely associated with healthy functioning and performance (Maltby et al., 2001; Neff, 2003). Studies have suggested that they both may involve similar mechanisms in impacting health (Conway-Williams, 2015, 2015).

Schulz et al. (2007) have found that compassion occurs when (a) there are affectional ties between two individuals, (b) there is an awareness of suffering, (c) the awareness generates distress and negative affect in the observer, and (d) the motivation of the observer to reduce or eliminate the observed suffering. Likewise, Mills et al. (2018) revealed that a lack of knowledge of the efficacy of compassion-based interventions may be behind its underuse in promoting self-care and enhancement practices. In essence, a better understanding and insight of compassion research may also have significant implications in palliative care practice and education. Self-compassion is not the same as self-forgiveness. The biggest difference between self-forgiveness and self-compassion is that self-forgiveness is episodic in nature, while self-compassion is an ongoing and active process. To exercise self-forgiveness, the individual must have committed some kind of perceived wrongdoing. In contrast, self-compassion is a dynamic practice in which an individual constant cultivates it regardless of any wrongdoings. Self-forgiveness is understood as a willingness to abandon self-blame and guilt following one's transgression while cultivating benevolence and compassion towards oneself (Ingersoll-Dayton & Krause, 2005).

1.1 Nature and Dynamics of Compassion

Compassion is a virtue essential for all. It is a basic force behind all heroic and altruistic deeds. Compassion is a natural attribute but requires a perception of the seriousness of the conditions caused by unjust fate, empathy and relatedness with the current dilemma (Cassell, 2009). Social relationships and connections denote the essential ingredients of a meaningful life and healthy adjustment (Seppala et al., 2012). These social relationships need to have and show concerns and care for others (Kashdan & Ciarrochi, 2013). Compassion is positively associated with positive life outcomes such as self-esteem, and academic achievements (Johnson et al., 1998) and longevity (Lum & Lightfoot, 2005). Compassion helps to feel better about ourselves and facilitate psychological health, well-being, forgiveness and resilience (Neff, 2011).

It also helps to improve from physical illness (Lown et al., 2017) and, thus, it has been labelled as the essence of nursing (Chambers & Ryder, 2009). Research has suggested compassion to benefit individuals in many ways. For example, compassion promotes social relationships, self-esteem, empathy, well-being; and higher interpersonal orientation (Seppala et al., 2012), increased happiness (Shapira & Mongrain, 2010), a higher level of well-being (Zessin et al., 2015) and improved adjustment (Ironson et al., 2017). Compassion for other and self-compassion facilitate higher satisfaction and lower distress (Lelorain et al., 2012), decreased anxiety (Fogarty et al., 1999), better self-control (Shepperd et al., 2015), lower self-criticism (Leaviss & Uttley, 2015), better parent-child relationships (Duncan et al., 2009), increased cooperation and learning (Hart et al., 2004), job satisfaction, organizational commitment, and sense of emotional vigour (Eldor & Shoshani, 2016), improved health (Lum & Lightfoot, 2005), optimism (Shapira & Mongrain, 2010), readiness to change (Kelly et al., 2010), positive ageing (Phillips & Ferguson, 2013) and buffers the negative impact of stress (Allen & Leary, 2010). On the other hand, compassion is also negatively linked with reduced PTSD symptom severity (Thompson & Waltz, 2008), psychopathological symptoms (MacBeth & Gumley, 2012), depression (Ehret et al., 2015) and burnout (Mills & Chapman, 2016).

Compassion for others is desirable virtue which involves the expression of kindness, a sense of common humanity, mindfulness, and reduced indifference toward the suffering of others (Pommier et al., 2020) and thus, It involves a caring attitude and behaviours as well as a desire to lower the sufferings (Goetz et al., 2010). Buddhist philosophy views compassion as an extension of human wisdom which help to become aware mindfully with the sufferings of others, experience of a set of kind responses and a strong feeling of relationships with others (Feldman, 2005; Jinpa, 2016). Compassion for others involves three dimensions: kindness-indifference, common humanity-separation and mindfulness-disengagement in response concerning others' sufferings (Pommier et al., 2020). Kindness represents being caring toward others who are facing pain and aims to support them. Common humanity comprises recognition of universal sufferings of all human beings and a sense of relationship with sufferers and sufferings. Mindfulness involves an unbiased awareness which helps to recognize the existence of the sufferings and their unavoidability.

Compassion for others has been suggested to be rooted in evolution (Goetz et al., 2010) which is evolved to extend support and caregiving to vulnerable offspring and promotes cooperative relations among individuals. It has been suggested that compassion for others represents a set of emotions which get activated in the face of the perceptions of sufferings of others and motivates its bearers to help the person in need. It is also assumed as a set of traits which involve the tendency to experience compassion across time and context (Goetz et al., 2010).

On the other hand, self-compassion comprises of a set of constructive attitudes towards one's self which becomes active after perceived pain, failures, adversities and inadequacies by individuals. Neff (2003) has proposed the most accepted self-compassion model that contains three mutual and interdependent bipolar components: self-kindness-self-judgement, common humanity-isolation and mindfulness-over-identification. The first aspect entails behaving oneself with a caring, warm and positive manner instead of harshly criticizing. Common humanity reflects seeing one's sufferings and painful experiences as a part of larger human realities rather than isolating from them. Mindful helps to maintain a balanced awareness of the failures and painful experiences to resolve them effectively rather than over-identifying with them (Neff, 2003; Pommier et al., 2020). A variety of positive life outcomes have been reported to be closely associated with self-compassion for people across age groups and socio-cultural affiliations (Neff, 2009, 2011; Pandey et al., 2019; Pommier et al., 2020).

1.2 Nature and Dynamics of Forgiveness

Forgiveness is also well-familiar and equally desirable human virtue which carries significant values for human survival and well-being. Traditionally, forgiveness has been assumed the subject matter of religion, philosophy and theology (Bobocel et al., 2019; Enright et al., 2020; Enright & Song, 2020; Madsen et al., 2009). The Positive Psychology movement has catalyzed a sudden increased interest in the scientific study of forgiveness (Legaree et al., 2007). Dictionary meaning says that forgiveness is giving up resentment against or the desire to punish, stop being angry with, to pardon or to give up all claims to punish or exact penalty for an offence (Merriam-Webster Dictionary, 2019). Studies have shown that forgiveness facilitates individuals to grant complete absolution and redemption, helps to free from past bitterness and promotes well-being, positive relationships and well-being (Epstein et al., 1998).

Forgiveness cultivates internal harmony, reparative strength, compassion, positive emotional and cognitive frameworks, health outcomes, well-being, and useful relationships for people of all age groups (Ahirwar et al., 2019; Demertzis, 2020; Pandey et al., 2020; Toussaint et al., 2015; Tuck & Anderson, 2014; Woodyatt et al., 2017). It also promotes positive health behaviours and social support for individuals, groups, organisations and communities (Tuck & Anderson, 2014; Woodyatt et al., 2017) due to its intrinsic attributes of reparative ability, resilience, successful coping and improved self-acceptance (Maynard et al., 2016). Forgiveness involves positive emotions that may directly fortify physical and psychological health by shaping perceptions, attributions and physiological processes of its practitioners (Davis et al., 2015; Enright et al., 2020; Karner-Huţuleac, 2020; Toussaint et al., 2015; Woodyatt et al., 2017). On the hand, forgiveness also helps to reduce psychopathological symptoms such as depression, anxiety and suicidal behaviours of individuals (Barcaccia et al., 2020; Hirsch et al., 2011; Nsamenang et al., 2013; Wulandari & Megawati, 2020).

There are differences in the opinions regarding the meaning of forgiveness. For example, some researchers have conceptualized forgiveness as a response whereas others have explained it as a personality disposition or a characteristic of social units (McCullough & Witvliet, 2002). Forgiveness has been suggested to be a pro-social change in a victim's thoughts, emotions, and/or behaviours toward transgressors (McCullough & Witvliet, 2002). This conceptualization includes entire positive changes in cognitive, affective and behavioural aspects of forgivers when they resolve to forgive transgressors for their wrongdoings (Mccullough & Worthington, 1994; Scobie & Scobie, 1998). Forgiveness, in terms of personality trait, may be conceived as an inclination to forgive others in a variety of interpersonal situations that may be reflected through forgiving-unforgiving continuum (Mullet et al., 1998).

Forgiveness has also been defined as a quality of social units that entails an attribute similar to intimacy, trust, or commitment related to popular social structures such as marriages, families, or communities that either facilitate or inhibit it (McCullough & Witvliet, 2002). Thompson et al. (2005) have defined forgiveness as a process which frees one from a negative affiliation with the cause of transgression that has acted against a person. According to Enright et al. (1998), forgiveness entails one's desire to give up anger, negative perceptions and unconcerned behaviour toward transgressors who have hurt the transgressed and development of compassion, kindness, and love toward the transgressors. According to McCullough et al. (2000), forgiveness involves motivation with a pro-social orientation which helps to soothe

the desire to avoid the transgressors and to hurt or seek vengeance on one hand and catalyse a strong desire to act and behave positively toward the wrongdoers. Rye et al. (2000) have argued for two aspects of forgiveness: the absence of negative emotion and presence of positive emotion towards the transgressors. Thus, forgiveness represents the expression of altruism and moral response from the side of transgressed that victim desires to replace unfairness with goodness. It is explicit that forgiveness is a complex process that involves a set of cognitive, affective and behavioural attributes which decrease negative attachment with transgression, transgressor and the transgressing situations. Forgiveness promotes compassion, generosity, pro-social behaviours and love toward, decreased revenge, positive behaviour, positive emotions, positive attribution frame and moral response towards the transgressors.

Researchers have proposed a variety of forgiveness. The decisional type refers to an intention of the forgivers to behave in a more benevolent manner, to remove negative behaviour and to restore positive behaviour with the transgressors (Exline et al., 2003; Finkel et al., 2002; McCullough et al., 2003). The emotional forgiveness involves changes in thoughts and feelings toward the transgressor, transgressions and the situations that are assumed to cause negative emotionality and facilitates negative emotions with positive ones.

Forgiveness may also be unconditional, conditional, the dismissive and grace types (The Good Men Project, 2019). Unconditional forgiveness is given for one's wrongdoings with taking into account one's faults with no conditions attached to it and assuming that the transgression never happened as such. Conditional forgiveness is a 'trust but verify' type that involves regular watch on the behaviours of the transgressor. It is given in the condition where the trust has not well built. Dismissive forgiveness represents an uncertain attitude towards transgressor and moving positively in their life of forgivers. Grace type involves that God is the ultimate forgiver and forgiveness is granted (The Good Men Project, 2019).

According to Walrond-Skinner (1998), forgiveness may be classified into seven major categories. Premature instantaneous is a forged type in which forgiveness is either forbidden or wrongdoings are forgotten. An arrested type of forgiveness takes place between the transgressor and the forgiver. Confessions, acceptance of transgressions and desirable alterations in behaviour lead to a conditional type of forgiveness. Pseudo or mutual forgiveness involves half-hearted forgiveness intending to reinstate pre-conflict relationships. Collusive forgiveness is the process of avoiding further conflict even in the face of unresolved and harsh unfairness. Repetitious type of forgiveness reflects half-hearted efforts to end interpersonal wrongdoings. Likewise, authentic process forgiveness entails a set of processes which motivates a person to avoid revengeful behaviours for benefitting others and self. It is guided by an unconditional, selfless and pro-social motive (Kj, 2018; Walrond-Skinner, 1998).

Enright et al. (1989) have proposed six major types of forgiveness. The first type is revengeful forgiveness that occurs after an offence while restitutional forgiveness is characterized by the lightening of guilt following the bringing back to a relationship. The third type is expectational forgiveness that is observed in perceived social pressure and the fourth type is known as lawful expectational forgiveness that is granted ensuing the moral code of authority. The fifth type is forgiveness for social harmony that is observed to maintain the present social harmony and peace while the sixth type denotes forgiveness as an act and expression of unconditional love (Enright et al., 1989; Kj, 2018).

Forgiveness has been popularized in family therapy perspective that focuses on relational ethics with its role in maintaining independence and relationships among family members (Hargrave, 1994). (Hargrave (1994) conceptualizes that the process of forgiveness occurs through exoneration and behaviour. This perspective assumes that insight and understanding are two significant aspects of forgiveness. On the one hand, insight helps one to become familiar with and modify one's disparaging pattern of thought and behaviour. On the other hand, understanding helps one to accept the weaknesses and limitations of wrongdoer without exterminating the responsibility (Hargrave, 1994).

Another approach provides that forgiveness may occur in interpersonal, self and situation. Interpersonal forgiveness has been studied extensively that occurs in the relationship between two or more individuals who are affected by verbal, behavioural, emotional or perceived transgression. For example, it may happen in interpersonal transgressions such as breaking the trust of a life partner, friend or some important family member. Worthington (1998) has proposed a REACH (recall, empathy, altruism, commit and hold) model of forgiveness that involves recalling offence, promoting empathy between the transgressed and transgressor, giving absolution as an unselfish souvenir to both the parties, committing and holding on forgiveness.

Forgiveness has evolved as a cognitive mechanism which is vital to establish, maintain and restore valuable social relationships for human beings (McCullough et al., 2011). A secure attachment pattern predicts dispositional forgiveness and reduces rumination (Burnette et al., 2007). Forgiveness is characterized by non-restriction, easiness and immediacy which make it most suitable for building and maintaining close interpersonal and social relationships.

Self-forgiveness involves a course of action which helps to reduce abhorrence towards the self in the face of perceived explicit wrongdoings (Wohl et al., 2008). Hall and Fincham (2005) have argued that it is more difficult for a person to live without self-forgiveness than without interpersonal forgiveness. This may be due to

the reason that lack of self-forgiveness may lower self-esteem, psychological well-

being and may lead to psychopathological symptoms of anxiety, suicide and

depression, poor social relationships. Conversely, the damage caused by lack of

interpersonal forgiveness may be limited to decreased external positive interaction

and adaptation. Moreover, it requires more efforts to face and deal with the negative

outcomes of shame in comparison to guilt since the former entails a generalized view

than the latter (Tangney et al., 2005). Self-forgiveness can be achieved by helping

people to understand the wrongdoings without preconceived notion, confess the

nature and role of internal and external factors and helping them to release hard

feelings without harming the self and psychological well-being (Snyder et al., 2011).

Situational forgiveness may be linked to natural disasters such as floods and

earthquakes or misfortunes of personal life such as untimely demise of loved ones or

prolonged incurable infirmity. These negative natural or man-made ill-conditions

cause people to become easily irritated and desperate and make them unforgiving

towards them. These negative attitudes, feelings and thinking towards situations may

result in hopelessness, emotional problems, anxiety and depression (Exline et al.,

1999).

The dynamic process model of forgiveness (Ho & Fung, 2011) assumes that

people with dissimilar cultural backgrounds differ in their motivational frameworks

and conceptualizations of forgiveness (Girard & Mullet, 1997; Kadiangandu et al.,

2007; McCullough & Witvliet, 2002). Moreover, forgiveness involves a change in

cognitions, emotions, and behaviours about transgressor, transgression and situation

(Enright & Fitzgibbons, 2015). Thus, the basic task in forgiveness is to change one

from a negative direction to positive ones in all these dimensions in a temporal continuum. In other words, emotions play an important role in forgiveness. It has been suggested that replacing negative emotions by positive ones through regulating emotions is the key to forgiveness (Kadiangandu et al., 2007). The forgiveness and emotion regulation processes are shaped by cultural realities.

1.3 Nature and Dynamics of Well-being

Well-being represents a set of experiences concerning health, happiness and affluence. It includes positive mental health, higher life satisfaction, a sense of meaning or purpose in life, and the capability to manage life stress. Research has provided for a variety of theoretical explanations of well-being. According to Fredrickson and Losada (2005), well-being comprises four characteristics viz., goodness, generativity, growth, and resilience. Hone et al. (2014) have reported four theoretical lines of thinking on well-being: Keyes (2002), Huppert and So (2013), Diener et al. (2010) and Seligman (2011). Keyes (2002) has suggested that the presence of higher emotional, psychological and social well-being is key components of well-being. The emotional well-being further involves positive affect and life satisfaction while psychological well-being denotes useful relationships, purpose in life, self-acceptance, environmental mastery, personal growth and autonomy. Lastly, the social well-being represents social contribution, social integration, social growth, social acceptance and social coherence (Keyes, 2005).

The conceptualization of well-being of Huppert and So (2013) was based on a thorough study of Diagnostic and Statistical Manual of Mental Disorders (American Psychiatric Association, 2013) and the International Classification of Diseases (World Health Organization, 1993). These researchers came up with competence, emotional stability, engagement, meaning, optimism, positive emotion, positive relationships, resilience, self-esteem, and vitality as the core features of well-being. These attributes of well-being were further refined by the statistical analysis which led to the development of three major components such as positive characteristics (emotional stability, vitality, optimism, resilience, and self-esteem), positive functioning (engagement, competence, meaning, and positive relationships), and positive appraisal (life satisfaction and positive emotion) and further identified hedonic and eudaimonic dimensions (Hone et al., 2014). This model has been a great precursor in assessing the well-being of many nations.

The well-being model of Diener et al. (2010) has been derived from the study of the models of well-being proposed by Ryan and Deci (2001) and Ryff (1989) who argued that humans have a set of needs which are universal and essential for effective functioning. It has been suggested that competence, self-acceptance, meaning and relatedness, optimism, giving and engagement have a significant role in well-being (Seligman, 2006). Similarly, Seligman (2011) has proposed that positive emotions, engagement, relationships, meaning in life and accomplishments are basic components of human well-being.

The study of well-being represents a promising new area of research with strong implications on inter-disciplinary orientation in its study approach. The study of well-being has significant implications in all areas of human life. For example, it is equally significant to personal, social, professional and work-life in all institutional contexts. Well-being has been observed to be closely associated with a host of positive life outcomes and human functioning across age and gender. The positive emotions catalyse the occurrence of useful cognition and strengthen adaptive behavioural patterns which consolidate performance, skills, creativity and insight on one hand and promote health and well-being on the other (Fredrickson & Losada,

2005). It may also promote self-efficacy, positive attitudes, and pro-social behaviours. Thus, understanding the nature and correlates of well-being is significant for the achievement of personal, community, organizational, societal and national goals.

1.4 Interdependent Happiness and its Dynamics

Happiness refers to a higher frequency of positive emotions and a lower frequency of negative emotions (Kitayama & Markus, 2000). In this sense, happiness is a universal experience but it may be embedded in particular socio-cultural contexts and situations. For example, the happiness of Americans may derive from personal achievements and favourable evaluation of self. Conversely, happiness for people in Eastern culture has its genesis from social harmony, interdependence and positive relationships. The dissimilar sources of happiness for people of different cultures may have their origin in historical ideologies, values and religious practices (Uchida et al., 2004). For European-American people, happiness is derived from personal achievement and the Protestant worldview which assumes self as worthy and competent to the intent of God. This belief in self-worth may be the source of happiness for them (Kitayama & Markus, 2000). On the other hand, happiness for the Eastern people may originate from the achievement of social harmony and balance among a variety of selves (Suh, 2002). Here, personal achievement may lead to negative interpersonal and social consequences and thus, positive and negative aspects of happiness may act as complementary to each other (Ji et al., 2001). Thus, it may be argued that happiness in European-American people may be viewed as personal achievement whereas the same may reflect social harmony and interdependence for people from the Eastern culture (Diener et al., 1995; Uchida et al., 2004). This may also be due to the differences in the construal of self which is interdependent and other-oriented (Uchida et al., 2004).

To explain these differences in the nature and dynamics of happiness for people of different cultural affiliations, researchers have conceptualized a new construct known as interdependent happiness for people with collective cultural values. Whereas happiness for people of European-American culture is based on person-focused achievements (Uchida et al., 2004), freedom of choices (Markus & Kitayama, 2010), easy expression of emotions (Matsumoto et al., 2008), mutual confirmation of positive attributes (Kitayama & Markus, 2000), the happiness of people brought up in Eastern societies may lend their genesis from other-oriented emotions such as friendly and positive feelings for other persons (Kitayama et al., 2006), affiliation with others, social harmony, the absence of emotional disturbance, transcendental reappraisal (Uchida & Kitayama, 2009) and interdependent goals (Oishi & Diener, 2001). It is explicit that interdependent goals are important for people in Eastern cultures (Uchida & Ogihara, 2012; Uchida et al., 2004) which shape the very nature of happiness. Contrary to the conceptualization of happiness in the individualistic societies as a global and subjective experience (Lyubomirsky & Lepper, 1999), the happiness of people of collectivistic culture may be construed as a close ally of life goals (Markus & Kitayama, 1991; Uchida & Kitayama, 2009). Thus, interdependent happiness may include subjective aspects as well as relationships. These researchers denied interdependent happiness as a global construct as its basic constituents such as interpersonal harmony, quiescence and ordinariness are peculiar to the societies professing collectivistic values where people live a collective way of life (Hitokoto & Uchida, 2015). Studies have suggested that interdependent orientation significantly shapes the health and well-being of individuals (Kitayama et al., 2010; Uchida & Oishi, 2016). A cross-cultural study indicated that interdependent happiness provides for the nourishment to positive life outcomes and is very relevant to explain a plethora of functioning and performance. It was reported that age is a positive correlate of interdependent happiness and it has been suggested that much is to be done to explicate its nature and dynamics (Hitokoto & Takahashi, 2020).

CHAPTER - 2
REVIEW OF LITERATURE

REVIEW OF LITERATURE

Forgiveness and compassion denote desirable human virtues which have been the subject matter of religion and philosophy for long. With the emergence of positive psychology, these constructs have recently gained popularity among scientists. Forgiveness occurs in response to the wrongdoings towards self and others which is more frequent and continuous. On the other hand, compassion consists of compassion for others and self-compassion. Forgiveness and compassion are efficacious in benefitting both the givers and receivers. The spontaneity and continuity make them important for understanding well-being and happiness. In essence, intrapersonal and interpersonal dimensions of forgiveness and compassion carry significance for well-being relationship and happiness.

2.1 Compassion and Well-being

Self-compassion has been defined as a set of positive self-attitudes, beliefs and behaviours that emerge and get activated in the face of perceived pain, adversity, personal inadequacies and genuine failures of life (Neff, 2003; Neff et al., 2018). Self-compassion entails of three bipolar constituents: self-kindness vs. self-judgement, common humanity vs. isolation and mindfulness vs. over-identification (Neff, 2003). It is a common fact that everybody faces challenges in their life and commits some mistakes (common humanity) which require acting in a manner that involves kindness and understanding of these feelings and actions (self-kindness). Moreover, the awareness of these sufferings (mindfulness) is the key to become self-compassionate (Neff, 2003; Neff et al., 2018). Findings suggest that those who are more frequently compassionate to others and themselves are less likely to have mental health problems and are more likely to report higher life satisfaction, more effective coping skills and to be higher in emotional intelligence (Barnard & Curry, 2011; Pandey et al., 2019). It has been suggested that self-compassion can be cultivated through proper interventions that may enhance the well-being of individuals (Leary et al., 2007). Self-compassionate interventions have been found to lower self-attacking and self-critical ways of relating to oneself (Gilbert & Irons, 2004) and increase self-compassion and self-reported well-being (Neff & Germer, 2017).

It has been argued that self-compassion facilitates mental health and well-being, which, in turn, makes it easier to cope with challenging life circumstances and eases emotion regulation. Certain challenges have been identified to cultivate self-compassion. For example, research with clinical populations suggests that people with mental health problems reported difficulties in learning self-compassionate behaviours because of a long-standing history of being unkind to themselves and their experiences of anxiety and depression that make it impossible for them to show kindness towards themselves (Pauley & McPherson, 2010). Gilbert et al. (2011) reported that clients often seem to be fearful of receiving compassion from others as well as from themselves. Together, these studies suggest that, within clinical settings, clients may experience compassion as threatening and find self-compassion difficult to occur. Self-compassion satisfaction refers to a positive feeling of individuals associated with knowing that they have helped themselves. The positive equilibrium caused by self-compassion results in increased flourishing (Mills & Chapman, 2016). Thus, self-compassion is beneficial for positive mental health and well-being (Pandey et al., 2019; Tiwari et al., 2020).

Spikins et al. (2010) have argued that self-compassion may have evolved as a means for furthering social relationships and adaptability. They further argued that self-compassion may have developed as a means of survival (Spikins et al., 2010). It has been suggested that with the process of evolution people have come to thrive on the sensations and they associate with being compassionate to self, others and having others be compassionate to them. In this manner, this sense of affiliation has become one method for regulating affect of human beings (Gilbert, 2004). Moreover, being compassionate to self and others also makes people vulnerable to exploitation that may incite their threat system and impacts their affective states. It has been argued that human beings have to balance their need for compassion with the need for self-protection and the drive to further one's interests (Gilbert, 2004). The benefit of self-compassion has proliferated to the other fields of human functioning. For example, organizations have started emphasizing the importance of creating a business-wide ethos of care and a system that notices, experiences and responds to suffering (Kanov et al., 2004; Lawrence & Maitlis, 2012). Rynes et al. (2012) have suggested that modelling compassionate and caring interactions are critical in developing an ethos of care in an organization.

Gilbert (2005, 2010) has suggested some key qualities of self-compassion. These include the motivation to be caring, sensitive, being able to be moved by distress, and being able to tolerate distress and understand it. It has been argued that human beings are a profoundly social species who depend on the safety, care, support, affection and encouragement of others to survive and thrive (Gilbert, 2005, 2010). These attributes also help to cultivate self-compassion and other self-resources (Gilbert, 2005, 2010). Some theoretical models of well-being have been proposed to explain the relationship between self-compassion and positive life outcomes (Diener & Ryan, 2009; Zessin et al., 2015). Goal theories suggest that well-being is the consequence of goal achievement. Self-compassion helps to attain goals of life by reducing the negative emotional consequences of inadequacies and failures (Barnard

& Curry, 2011; Emmons, 1986). Two cognitive approaches to well-being have been proposed to understand the nature of the association between self-compassion and well-being: top-down and bottom-up theories. Top-down theories explain the development of well-being through a positive memory bias and the influence of personality (Diener & Biswas-Diener, 2008). In other words, a person with a strong sense of well-being focuses more on positive situations and interprets events more positively in consideration of pleasant memories. With a positive mindset, individuals would focus less on their own mistakes and failures with harsh and negative emotional thoughts and more on positive memories (Diener & Ryan, 2009).

Bottom-up theories assume a balancing process between the positive and negative experiences of a person that facilitates the achievement of well-being (Diener & Ryan, 2009). Thus, evaluations of positive situations increase well-being while understanding negative situations decrease the level of well-being. According to the cognitive approach, self-compassion does not directly contribute to well-being. It only helps to make a balance between positive and negative experiences (Zessin et al., 2015). Another approach is known as adaption theory, set-point theory or hedonic treadmill that explains well-being with the past as a standard for comparison of individuals (Diener et al., 2006; Diener & Ryan, 2009; Lucas, 2007). This theory assumes that the level of well-being of individuals changes temporarily when conditions of living alter.

Spandler and Stickley (2011) have argued that an understanding of self-compassion is necessary to appreciate mental health and human relationships. It has been argued that self-compassion may be facilitated through nurturing and healing environments. The recognition of the importance of healing family and social environments is important. Most of the earlier studies have focused on the study of self-compassion on individual perspective. The study of the relationship between self-compassion and well-being of married couples is very limited (Podvoll, 1990; Sedgwick, 1982). The researchers have reported that compassion can be facilitated or significantly inhibited within different social and cultural value systems (Bunting, 2004). Self-compassion seems to be beneficial for individuals' psychological well-being. The relationship between self-compassion and psychological well-being has been largely explored through survey methods in previous studies. High self-compassion is associated with reduced stress, anxiety, and depressive symptoms (MacBeth & Gumley, 2012). Self-compassion is also related to the improvements in self-reported indicators of positive affectivity, such as greater happiness, optimism, positive affect, and life satisfaction (Neff, 2003; Neff et al., 2007). It has been reported that the individuals who are more compassionate towards others could be more compassionate towards themselves (Breines & Chen, 2013; Neff & Pommier, 2013). Recent evidence suggests that the positive (common humanity, mindfulness and self-kindness) and negative (isolation, over-identification and self-judgment) components of Neff's conceptualization measure distinct constructs and can better be used separately as measures of self-compassion and self-coldness, respectively (Breines & Chen, 2013; López et al., 2018; Muris et al., 2018; Neff & Pommier, 2013).

Lopez et al. (2018) have suggested that the compassion for others and self-compassion are independent constructs and should be studied separately. Self-compassion is more strongly related to negative and positive indicators of an affect than compassion for others. Compassion for others is higher in women than in men, and in low educated individuals compared to higher educated individuals. In contrast, self-compassion is lower in low educated individuals. It has been suggested that compassion for others evolved as part of a caregiving response to vulnerable offspring, that it promotes cooperative relations between non-kin, and that compassionate mate are preferred. Compassion for others and self-compassion seem to be beneficial for individuals' psychological well-being. The evidence for the association of compassion for others and well-being comes primarily from experimental and intervention studies. Community adults that performed a daily compassionate action towards others in a 1-week task study showed increases in self-reported happiness at the end of the week, compared to a control condition (Mongrain et al., 2011). A small significant association between compassion for others and self-compassion has been observed (Breines & Chen, 2013; Neff & Pommier, 2013). Self-compassion has been found to be significantly related to depressive symptoms, negative affect, and positive affect (MacBeth & Gumley, 2012; Neff, 2003a; Neff et al., 2007). Compassion for others is significantly related to positive affect (Jazaieri et al., 2014; Mongrain et al., 2011).

Previous studies have reported gender difference in compassion in undergraduate students, community adults, and meditators (Neff & Pommier, 2013; Stellar et al., 2012). The social role theory of helping behaviours (Eagly & Crowley, 1986) suggests that gender roles encourage males to perform heroic actions while females to be nurturing and caring. The researchers have reported no gender differences in self-compassion, similarly to results from a study among undergraduates, community adults, and meditators (Neff & Pommier, 2013). A recent meta-analysis, however, found slightly lower self-compassion in women compared to men, as measured by the SCS total score (Yarnell et al., 2015). Low-educated individuals reported higher compassion for others compared to their counterparts. Similarly, previous research found that lower-class individuals reported greater compassion for others during laboratory inductions and real social interactions, compared to upper-class individuals (Stellar et al., 2012). Gilbert (2005, 2010) has argued that compassion is not only felt for close others but also for unfamiliar people. Gilbert (2010) conceptualizes compassion for others not only as being aware of and moved by suffering and wanting to help but also as the ability to adopt a non-judgmental stance towards others and to tolerate one's own distress when faced with other people's suffering.

2.2 Self-Compassion and Happiness

Self-compassion represents one of the promising self-resources having preventive and promotive strengths with significant relevance to maintain harmony with the internal and external realities of life for individuals (Tiwari et al., 2020). Unlike self-esteem, self-compassion has no negative outcomes for its holders (Neff, 2011). Neff (2003a) conceptualized self-compassion as a set of positive self-attitudes that get activated during pain, failures, adversities and inadequacies of life. Self-compassion facilitates self-understanding, understanding of suffering as a common fact, focus on the present, ease release of a chain of positive and incessant energy emanating from the core of self and successfully inhibit judgemental, harsh and critical attitude. Self-kindness helps to improve warmth, unconditional self-acceptance, useful self-love and non-productive self-criticism. Common humanity encourages realization of shared human experiences, broadens realities of life, connectedness, imperfections and errors of life. Mindfulness facilitates awareness of a momentary aspect of present experiences that enhance clarity and balance of human sufferings. Thus, self-compassion helps to achieve and maintain a potential understanding of self, experiences, diverse life conditions, usualness of human suffering, inner focus, an efficacious attribution style and other positive cognitions (Tiwari et al., 2020). Self-compassion helps to understand and explain success/failures of life, the significance of meaning in life, connectedness and cooperation that may eventually lead an individual to achieve hedonic and eudaimonic well-being (Barnard & Curry, 2011; Pandey et al., 2019; Pandey et al., 2020; Ryan & Deci, 2001).

Many positive life outcomes have been linked with self-compassion. For example, self-compassion shows positive relationships with well-being (Muris et al., 2018; Pandey et al., 2019; Verma & Tiwari, 2017), life satisfaction (Barnard & Curry, 2011; Bluth et al., 2016), social connectedness (Williams et al., 2008), emotional intelligence (Neff, 2003b), happiness (Neff, 2003a), an optimistic outlook (Yamaguchi et al., 2014; Zessin et al., 2015) and positive mental health (Rai & Tiwari, 2019; Tiwari et al., 2020). Conversely, self-compassion exhibits negative associations with anxiety, negative affect, depression, stress and other mental health issues (López et al., 2015; MacBeth & Gumley, 2012; Pfattheicher et al., 2017).

Many mechanisms have been suggested behind the positive impacts of self-compassion. For example, self-compassion has been suggested to promote resilience and community orientation (Akin & Akin, 2015; Tanaka et al., 2011) as well as thriving positive emotions, positive behaviours, acceptance and positive attributions (Barnard & Curry, 2011). Self-compassionate people use language that reflects connection rather than isolation (Neff et al., 2007). In addition, self-compassionate people exhibit higher levels of feelings of autonomy, competence, relatedness and self-determination (Magnus et al., 2010).

It is noticeable that self-compassion is one of the important sources of happiness. The majority of the American and Western researchers have conceptualized happiness as a subjective and emotionally arousing state juxtaposed with a higher frequency of positive emotions and lower occurrence of negative emotions (Fredrickson, 2001; Lyubomirsky & Lepper, 1999; Uchida & Oishi, 2016). Lyubomirsky and Lepper (1999) have defined happiness as a global and subjective assessment of whether one is a happy or unhappy person. Western culture conceptualizes happiness as the reflection of personal achievements (Uchida et al., 2004), free-choice (Markus & Kitayama, 2010), self-affirmation resources (Pandey et al., 2020; Tiwari et al., 2020), expression of emotions (Matsumoto et al., 2008) and reciprocated affirmation of internal positive strengths (Kitayama & Markus, 2000).

Conversely, happiness in collectivistic societies is characterized by connectedness and low arousal which is labelled as interdependent happiness (Markus & Kitayama, 1991; Oishi et al., 1999; Suh & Oishi, 2004; Uchida & Ogihara, 2012; Uchida & Kitayama, 2009). Happiness in people from collectivistic societies may be based on bond with others, friendly feelings toward others, ordinariness, interpersonal harmony, quiescence, interpersonally engaged emotions and interdependent goals (Kitayama et al., 2006; Oishi & Diener, 2001; Suh & Oishi, 2004; Uchida & Kitayama, 2009). The differences between the conceptualizations of happiness in the individualistic and collectivistic cultures may be guided by the dissimilar nature of self-construct which is culturally embedded (Kwan et al., 1997).

2.3 Forgiveness and Positive Life Outcomes

Many positive life outcomes have been suggested to be closely linked with forgiveness. Maltby et al. (2001) suggested that forgiveness represents a vital psychological construct having significant practical implications to underscore health and other important outcomes of human life. Mauger et al. (1992) argued that a failure to forgive oneself may lead to intro-punitive behaviours whereas failure to forgive others may result in extra-punitive behaviours and thus, may finally result into social alienation and social introversion (Maltby & Day, 2001). The findings also suggested that the concept of forgiveness is closely related to personality and psychological well-being variables and has implications for individual and social psychopathology.

Mauger et al. (1992) have argued that failure to forgive oneself is significantly positively correlated with depression, anxiety, distrust, self-esteem, and social introversion, while failure to forgive others is significantly positively correlated to schizophrenic traits, self-alienation and persecutory ideas. In addition, failure to forgive oneself and others both are significantly negatively correlated with social desirability (Mauger et al., 1992). It has also been suggested that lack of self-forgiveness is significantly related to aspects of negative aspects of psychological well-being such as higher depression and higher anxiety (Mauger et al., 1992). Lack of self-forgiveness may lead to neuroticism and anxiety while failure to forgive others may give rise to depression in a similar manner in males and females. Furthermore, failure to forgive others in extravert males results in depression while extraverted females show symptoms of psychoticism, anxiety and social dysfunction as a consequence of failure to forgive others (Bono et al., 2008; McCullough et al., 2007; Ryan & Deci, 2000; Wohl et al., 2008).

Assessing the role of forgiveness in marriage relationships, Fincham et al. (2002) have reported that forgiveness helps to restore relationships, release bitterness and anger, and heal inner emotional wounds (Diblasio & Proctor, 1993). The researchers have also observed that studies of forgiveness have recently mushroomed (McCullough et al., 1998), but little is known about forgiveness in marriage (Fenell, 1993; Fincham, 2000). Forgiveness is not directly related to the marital quality, affective reactions and emotional empathy but it indirectly catalyzes a chain of positive attributions which may result in improved marital relationships (Bradbury & Fincham, 1992). It has been demonstrated that attributions and emotional reactions are crucial in understanding their willingness to forgive the partners (Fincham, 2000). Attributions and behaviours exhibited during problem-solving and support discussions are more strongly related among wives than among husbands (Bradbury et al., 1996; Miller & Bradbury, 1995). Moreover, it was observed that wives engage in more attributional activity than husbands do (Holtzworth-Munroe & Jacobson, 1985). Wives are more sensitive to relationships (Worell, 1988). Fenell (1993) has reported that spouses believe that the willingness to forgive and be forgiven is one of the most important characteristics for marital satisfaction and longevity. McCullough et al. (1998) has also found that forgiving occurs more frequently in committed close relationships and forgiveness is closely linked with the restoration of closeness in marital relationships following an interpersonal transgression.

Forgiveness has been suggested to play an important role in human relationships of all sorts but its systematic empirical enquiry took a new momentum only after the establishment of Positive Psychology in 2000. Forgiveness involves intra-individual and pro-social change towards a perceived transgression situated in a specific interpersonal context (McCullough et al., 2001). Forgiveness catalyzes positive changes that involve willingness, consent and conscious decision of the forgivers (Worthington et al., 2007). Many benefits of observing and practising forgiveness have been reported by researchers. For instance, forgiveness is important to understand mental and physical health (Harris & Thoresen, 2005). According to Maltby et al. (2001), forgiveness is an central construct to understand many positive and significant outcomes of human life. Forgiveness is also helpful in achieving internal harmony and balance, empathetic understanding, positive cognition and emotion, reparative force, health outcomes, well-being, and close interpersonal and social relationships for children, adults and elders (Ahirwar et al., 2019; Pandey et al., 2020). Forgiveness has also been argued to be significant for a romantic relationship, marital longevity and satisfaction (Fenell, 1993). Forgiveness carries relevance in the healing of relationship transgressions involving betrayal (Gordon et al., 2005) and relationship hurts (Fincham et al., 2004). Forgiveness is positively associated with psychological well-being because it helps people preserve and reinstate lost relationships (Karremans et al., 2003). According to self-determination theory, forgiveness is linked with well-being as helps to influence the forgiver's perceptions of his or her relationship and connectedness with the transgressor (Reis et al., 2000).

It has been argued that successful marriage depends upon the forgiveness of couples (Worthington & Scherer, 2004). Forgiveness has been observed to play a facilitative role in facing current problems, avoiding new problems and to uphold the relationships of couples (Worthington & Scherer, 2004). It has been suggested that forgiveness can regain faith in a marital relationship in the face of contravention (Gordon et al., 2000). It is also important to understand the relationship between marital satisfaction (Fincham & Linfield, 1997), conflict and negative attributions, lowered loyalty, and non-empathetic attitudes in marital relationships (Fincham et al., 2006). Self-forgiveness helps to give up negative thoughts, feelings and behaviours and helps replace these with positive behaviours towards self (Enright, 1996). Self-forgiveness enables individuals to become aware and deal with their negative feelings. Self-forgiveness enhances well-being by helping people upholding good, useful and compassionate relationships (McCullough et al., 2000).

The above discussion makes it clear that forgiveness is a positive strength that helps replace negative cognitions, affects and behavioural outcomes with positive ones. It has been observed that forgiveness helps to reinstate fragmented relationships, lowers resentment and cures emotional injury arising out of worsened marital relationships (Fincham et al., 2002). In spite of the growing research on forgiveness, its role in the marriage relationship is not well-studied (Kearns & Fincham, 2004; McCullough et al., 1998). Thus, forgiveness carries relevance to underscore well-being and other life outcomes of individuals (Karremans et al., 2003). On the other hand, non-forgiving behaviours have been reported to be positively linked with psychopathological symptoms (Berry & Worthington, 2001). McCullough et al. (2001) have suggested that self-forgive helps individuals to make the feelings, actions and beliefs about their self more positive that make prompt them to think rationally and act constructively. Thus, self-forgiveness may also have significant relevance in close relationships as the nature of marriage relationships are regulated through attributions, emotional reactions and empathy.

Previous studies showed that forgiving people have been found to be able to reconstruct wrongdoings in a positive sequence of events about the offenders, offences and their consequences. Furthermore, it has been argued that forgiveness of self and situations may be crucial to understand the relationship between forgiveness of others and positive outcomes in marital relationships (Heinze & Snyder, 2001). Forgiveness may have a positive impact on marriage as it lowers psychological aggression and enhances constructive communication (Fincham et al., 2004). Forgiveness may carry relevance in marital relationships as it lowers retaliation and enhances benevolence (Fincham et al., 2004). Contrarily, un-forgiveness may carry forward the unsettled transgressions that may escalate future conflicts and negative interaction patterns leading to poor quality of marital relationships (Fincham et al., 2004).

2.4 Demographic Factors and Life Outcomes

The cultural context of Indian society is dissimilar to those of American and Western societies. Hindu cultural system assumes marriage as one of the sacraments that have worldly as well as eternal aspects. Hindu marriage is assumed to act as a means for people to achieve four *Purusharthas* of life namely *Dharma* (religion), *Artha* (worldly resources), *Kama* (sensual pleasure) and *Moksha* (salvation). For example, marriage helps to free an individual from *pitri rinas* (paternal debt) by giving birth to children. The ultimate goal of Hindu life is to achieve *Moksha* (salvation). It is the marriage that provides an opportunity for people to attain *Moksha* by *Dharma* (religion), *Artha* (worldly resources) and *Kama* (sensual pleasure). Thus, Hindu marriage is well-structured in its nature, practise and goals that are significantly different from marriage in other religions. Here in India, marriage relationships are generally arranged and are fixed by a set of familial and cultural rules considering genealogy and *Gotra* (lineage). Thus, marriage in India is well-institutionalized and based on a set of philosophical and religious principles. These attributes of Hindu marriage make it a unique system that significantly shapes the relationship of Hindu married couples.

Marriage is a union of two individuals. It has been argued that married people are happier than unmarried ones (Amato, 2009). It has been suggested that marriage enhances happiness through a set of its by-products such as the presence of children, positive relationships, security, meaningfulness and productive goals (Amato, 2009; Kamp Dush et al., 2008; Munsey, 2010). There are enough cultural differences, expectations and outcomes of married life among the societies of the world which make this issue remain relevant for a scientific inquiry. Hindu marriage is a *Sanskar* (sacrament) rather a contract between two individuals. It reflects a union of two families and not between two individuals. The husband has a more active role in worldly activities while the wife has a passive role. For a Hindu, marriage is essential to repay *Rinas* (debts) and achieve *Purusharthas* (object of human pursuit) such as *Dharma* (righteousness or moral values), *Kama* (pleasure), *Artha* (Worldly achievements) and *Moksha* (liberation). Wife is said to be *Ardhagini* (half of man). In essence, the Hindu marriage is characterized by its sacramental nature, irrevocability and a stronger union of mind, body and soul (Sharma et al., 2013). This unique nature of the relationship of ties in Hindu marriage cannot be found in any other marriage systems of the world. The nature of the marriage relationship between a husband and a wife is also unique. The basic goals of interpersonal harmony, social interactions and achievements of life have a specific meaning in Indian culture (Sharma et al., 2013). Unlike other religions, Hindu marriage is assumed as a religious sacrament which has been developed to attain a variety of eternal, spiritual and worldly goals of human life. The study of the relationship between self-compassion and well-being of married Hindu couples will through some new light on this issue as self-compassion is linked with emotional processes and goal achievement (Jazaieri et al., 2014; Mongrain et al., 2011).

Moreover, socio-cultural realities and traditional practices are facing incessant change in Indian society today. The joint family is being replaced with the nuclear family. Educational and employment opportunities are available to both the genders. In light of these changes, some characteristic changes in the marriage relationship may be expected. Indian society reflects the attributes of individualism and collectivism simultaneously (Sinha & Tripathi, 1994). Studies have shown that achievements and performance of Indian people is shaped and supported by both self-esteem (a construct relevant to individual dynamics of people brought up in individualistic societies) and self-compassion (helpful to underscore performance and behaviours of persons socialized in collectivistic values) (Pandey et al., 2019). It is evident that the studies are limited in understanding the nature and dynamics of the relationships among compassion (compassion for others and self-compassion), three aspects of forgiveness (forgiveness of self, forgiveness of others and forgiveness of situations) and well-being and interdependent happiness of married Hindu couples in the present incessantly altering socio-cultural milieu.

Family is a conglomeration of two or more people, who share the common shelter, habits and mutual goals and tied either by blood or marriage relationships. The institution of the family is universal and dynamic in nature and has many forms. The joint family system is more prevalent in collectivistic societies like India (Chadda & Deb, 2013) whereas the nuclear family is more popular in materially advanced societies like America (Ruggles, 2009). The various forms of families are characterized by size, generation, skills, experiences and personal as well as social goals. The characteristic features of different family systems may have relevance to understanding the dynamics of happiness. The family has been found to have a close link with happiness as family values are always kept on an upper hand over personal values which regulate the very construal of meaning, relationship, methods of living well, values pursuits, happiness and other life goals (Krys et al., 2019). Joint and nuclear families differ not only in their composition and structure but also in their functions and regulatory roles for individuals and society. A joint family is said to cultivate more mutuality, interdependence and adherence to religious and spiritual practices while a nuclear family promotes independence, preference for individual achievements, individual freedom and less observance to religious practices (Gautam, 2020; Pandey et al., 2020; Tiwari et al., 2020; Tiwari et al., 2020). Thus, understanding the role of the family in influencing well-being and interdependent happiness would constitute a significant contribution.

The social class may also impact the relationship between self-compassion and well-being of married couples. It is evident that lower social class is denoted by reduced material resources (lower-income, educational attainment) and subordinate social rank vis-a-vis others. Lacking resources and rank, lower-class individuals face harsher environments than their upper-class counterparts (Adler et al., 1994; Lareau, 2011) and these environments are theorized to shape emotional experiences. Lower-class individuals prove to be more emotionally reactive to ambiguous and negative social situations (Chen et al., 2004; Gallo et al., 2005; Kessler & Cleary, 1980; Matthews et al., 2010; Taylor & Seeman, 1999). Social class is a form of social hierarchy that arises from the number of material resources an individual possesses (Adler et al., 2000; Kraus & Keltner, 2009; Oakes & Rossi, 2003). Lower-class individuals develop in environments with greater threats and external obstacles (less-safe neighbourhoods, poorly funded educational institutions), and are less able to use their limited resources to overcome these obstacles (Gallo & Matthews, 2003). It has been argued that further research is needed to address this issue afresh to understand well the role of demographic and individual factors shaping the relationships among compassion (compassion for others and self-compassion), three facets of forgiveness (forgiveness of self- situations and others), well-being and interdependent happiness of married couples (Zessin et al., 2015).

In essence, socioeconomic status (SES) and other demographic factors have been found to influence the nature and extent of well-being and happiness of individuals. In a cross-national study of 15 countries, age, marital status, employment and other demographic factors are associated with the well-being and happiness and other emotional outcomes (Peiró, 2006). Socioeconomic status refers to the social standing of an individual in a group which includes income, occupation and education. It also reflects inequities in access to various resources, social privilege, power and control (Jain et al., 2018). A recent study has revealed that SES denotes a long-term influential factor relevant to explicate happiness and psychological well-being (Fassbender & Leyendecker, 2018). Consequent upon fast social and technological changes, many new socio-cultural attributes are added to human life which may alter the previous understanding of the association between SES, well-being and happiness. For example, the proliferation of education, new opportunities of employment, the role of mass media, new technology and social welfare policies have influenced the SES conditions of people in the recent past. A higher SES of an individual may increase the availability of material resources on one hand and decrease the availability of free-time and quality of close relationships on the other. It has been argued that SES factors have lasting impacts on personal and social identities of people and exert significant influence on their feelings, thoughts and behaviours (Manstead, 2018). In comparison to middle-class, lower-class individuals are more likely to have an interdependent self-concept, an immediacy in behaviours, a lower sense of personal control, a higher empathy and a more supportive attitude to others in distress (Manstead, 2018). In a recent study, well-being and happiness showed close relationships with gender, age, employment and marital status (Rothert et al., 2020).

Gender differences in well-being and happiness have also been observed. For example, women are happier than men but they also report a higher frequency of negative emotions. Men and women differ in their level of cooperation, interdependence, relationship orientation and responses to various social stimulations (Fujita et al., 1991). These gender differences may make them susceptible to experience dissimilar interdependent happiness. Men and women also differ in their gender stereotype, emotional expressions, social relations and the socialization of emotions which may make them experience different levels of happiness (Plant et al., 2000). Women more easily express their happiness, warmth and fear which make them develop stronger social bonding and caring than men. On the other hand, men more readily express anger, pride and contempt (Plant et al., 2000). Thus, the well-being and happiness of men and women may be guided by dissimilar mechanisms. For instance, the well-being and happiness of men are linked with living with family or spouse and occupation whereas positive relationships, care and interdependence have more relevance to understanding the well-being and happiness of women (Moriyama et al., 2018). The gender differences in well-being and happiness may be related to differences in emotion recognition, social sensitivity, self-esteem, close friendships, valuing emotions, achievement empathy and differential use of the areas of the brain (Chui & Wong, 2016; Moriyama et al., 2018; Schulte-Rüther et al., 2008; Wong et al., 2020). These differences in the psychological and physiological attributes may make women experience more happiness than men (Moriyama et al., 2018; Wong et al., 2020).

Education provides people with an opportunity to learn, explore and grow in life. It has been argued that individual and collective happiness and education are closely linked (Noddings, 2003). According to Layard (2006), seven factors are essential for happiness: family relationships, financial situation, work, community and friends, health, personal freedom and personal values. These all are achievable through proper education and thus, education has an indirect role in the happiness of people (Layard, 2006). There is disagreement about the relationship between age and happiness (Laaksonen, 2016; Wong et al., 2020). Some researchers argue that there is a U-shaped relationship between age and happiness and suggest happiness to occur minimum during the middle adulthood due to the multiplicity of life challenges as compared to the other developmental periods (Blanchflower & Oswald, 2008). Others suggest that happiness is the end result of health status, age, sex, region and socio-economic characteristics (Sun et al., 2016). Thus, the relationship between age and happiness is inconclusive and needs further investigation (Wong et al., 2020).

The above discussion makes it apparent that there is limited research showing the impacts of self-compassion and forgiveness on the well-being and interdependent happiness (Gerber et al., 2015). Likewise, the study of these constructs has been limited to some selected American, European and Asian countries (Hitokoto & Uchida, 2015). There are also limited studies of these constructs involving demographics such as age, gender, family (structure, size and composition), socioeconomic status and occupation. The Hindu married couples may be an especial case as Hindu marriage is a sacrament with acts as a means to fulfil worldly as well as spiritual needs through special religious and social provisions. The relationships and life goals of a Hindu married couple are more guided by specific religious and spiritual arrangements. The impacts of the postmodern lifestyle, the increasing role of mass media and materialistic values, new opportunities of social mobility and weakening of joint family system in Indian society may have changed the basic institution of Hindu marriage. The study of these constructs in the context of the unique features of the relationships of the Hindu married couples and current socio-cultural realities may help to understand their dynamics for well-being and interdependent happiness in a novel way. Thus, this study will help fill the gap pertaining to the limited research on compassion (compassion for others and self-compassion), forgiveness (forgiveness of self- situations and others), well-being and interdependent happiness with diverse populations and cultures, particularly because of the difference between individualistic and collectivistic conceptualizations of well-being and happiness.

CHAPTER - 3
RESEARCH METHODOLOGY

RESEARCH METHODOLOGY

3.1 Statement of the Problem

Review of literature suggests that intrapersonal and interpersonal attributes of compassion and forgiveness carry a significant role in shaping the well-being, interdependent happiness and mental health of the individuals. According to previous studies, the forgiveness of others correlates with self-compassion and doesn't correlate with self-forgiveness. But self-forgiveness and self-compassion are positively correlated with the well-being. Forgiveness of others and self-forgiveness are different constructs and they act differently for the well-being of the individuals. Hence, to understand the relationship between self-compassion and self-forgiveness and to the extent, these intrapersonal attributes explain well-being, further studies are essential.

It is also evinced from the studies that self-compassion predicts well-being. Self-compassion is a part of the personality which is present every time whereas self-forgiveness is episodic in nature, hence it can be argued that self-forgiveness may mediate the relationship between self-compassion and self-forgiveness. Individuals who score high on self-compassion are equally kind to others (Neff, 2003), and low on self-compassion are kinder to others than self (Neff, 2003; Neff & Germer, 2013). Forgiveness and compassion strengthen the bond of social connection and thus, they may impact close and positive relationship outcomes including well-being (Kimweli & Stilwell, 2002; Lee & Robbins, 1998).

There are many benefits associated with practising forgiveness and compassion. Forgiveness and compassion have been observed to enhance social activity that leads to satisfying social relationships and happiness (Diener &

Seligman, 2004), lower depression and anxiety, and increases resilience across a broad array of stressful life events and environments (Lee & Robbins, 1998). Wohl et al. (2008) have observed that self-forgiveness has an important role in shaping psychological well-being. McCullough et al. (2000) conceived forgiveness as a constellation of pro-social motivations. According to the Enright and The Human Development Study Group (1996), when people self forgive they are more likely to think, act constructively toward self and believe the self to be a worthy individual. Thompson et al. (2005) have found that forgiveness is positively related with positive affect and cognitive flexibility on one hand and shows negative association with reprisal, hostility, and rumination on the other. Forgiveness also have been suggested to closely shape and structure well-being, anxiety, depression, anger and life satisfaction. Conversely, unforgiveness demonstrates a positive relationship with perceived stress and a variety of psychopathological symptoms (Maltby et al., 2001; Mauger et al., 1992; Witvliet et al., 2001).

Several studies have shown that compassion increases interdependent happiness and positive emotions that, in turn, has been linked to a host of psychological benefits (Brown et al., 2019). Positive emotions help broaden resources and optimize performance such as intellectual resources (creativity and flexible thinking), social resources (ability to connect with others), physical resources (improved health and coordination) and psychological resources (Fredrickson, 2001). The relationship between compassion and self-compassion has not been well understood. It is argued that compassion for others and self-compassion is, in fact, part of the same overarching construct. While Buddhist thinking argues that differentiating compassion for others from self-compassion means drawing a false distinction between the self and others, and self-compassion is a prerequisite for showing 'true' compassion towards others.

There are many benefits of observing compassionate behaviours. Gilbert (2005, 2010) identifies key qualities of compassion such as the motivation to be caring, sensitive, being able to be moved by distress, and being able to tolerate distress and understand it. Compassion can be facilitated or significantly inhibited within different social and cultural value systems (Bunting, 2004). In essence, forgiveness and compassion have many positive outcomes for individuals. No systematic study has been conducted to underscore the relationships among these constructs with well-being and interdependent happiness. Forgiveness obtains its association with well-being precisely because forgiveness helps people maintain and restore close relationships (Karremans et al., 2003). A multitude of mechanisms has been put forward to explain the impacts of forgiveness on well-being and other positive outcomes. Findings suggest that forgiving people can reframe transgressions and construct a new narrative such that they are no longer beset by negative thoughts, feelings, or behaviours about the transgression, transgressor, and associated outcomes. Furthermore, many studies have indicated that forgiveness of self (Heinze & Snyder, 2001; Mauger et al., 1992) and situations (Heinze & Snyder, 2001) may be crucial domains for the relationship between forgiveness and well-being. Previous studies of forgiveness in couple relationship have ignored marriage relationship and most were confined to romantic relationships (McCullough et al., 1998). In addition, previous studies have been characterized by hypothetical scenarios of marital transgressions and relatively minor transgressions. As forgiveness helps to rebuild relationships by assisting the victim to let go of bitterness and anger and regain a realistic view of the partner, the assessment of their role in the well-being of married couples will be an important contribution (Gordon et al., 2000).

Maltby and Day (2001) suggested that there are gender differences in personality and psychological well-being correlates of forgiveness of others, but not in the forgiveness of self, and it is required to further explore why men and women differ in the forgiveness of others and are similar in their forgiveness of self. Worthington (1998) speculates on the differences between men and women in forgiveness, but the reasons behind these gender differences are not known. In addition, previous studies have employed the study of forgiveness independent of gender while studying couple relationships. As men and women differ in their responses to transgression and perception of relationship damages, further studies are needed to underscore the role of forgiveness and compassion in achieving well-being (Gonzales et al., 1994). Compassion for others was higher in women than in men, and in low educated individuals compared to higher educated individuals. In contrast, self-compassion was lower in low educated individuals. Future research can build upon these findings to enlarge the understanding of how compassion for others and self-compassion relate and differ from each other. Only a few studies have explored the relationship between compassion for others and self-compassion (Neff, 2003). A meta-analysis, however, found slightly lower self-compassion in women compared to men (Yarnell et al., 2015). Thus, there are contradictions in gender differences of forgiveness and compassion as well as their role in shaping various life outcomes. Socioeconomic status has been reported to be an important correlate of forgiveness and compassion. Stellar et al. (2012) have found that relative to their upper-class counterparts, lower-class individuals reported elevated dispositional compassion, as well as greater self-reported compassion during a compassion-inducing video and for another person during social interactions. On the other hand, lower-class individuals also exhibited heart rate deceleration (a physiological response associated with orienting to the social environment and engaging with others) during the compassion-inducing video.

A perusal of the findings of the previous studies highlights a lack of research exploring the relationships between forgiveness, self-forgiveness, self-compassion, compassion, well-being, and interdependent happiness of couples. Empathy, distress tolerance, and kindness are key attributes of compassion, with self-kindness associated with reduced self-criticism, blame and worry (Gilbert & Procter, 2006). It has been suggested that it would be important to further examine the association of compassion for others and self-compassion across different cultures and in younger populations that will enlarge the understanding of how compassion for others and self-compassion relate and differ from each other. Forgiveness of others and self are closely linked with well-being (Fisher & Exline, 2006). The basic features of self-compassion and self-forgiveness have been reported to closely similar since the former protects self-regard of individuals in the face of odds of human life. It is argued that the interrelationships of self-compassion and self-forgiveness remain underexplored yet. They have been conceptualized as pro-social and supportive resources relevant for self-regulation and act as a close ally of spirituality and other positive strengths of human beings (Mahoney et al., 2005; Neff et al., 2005; Witvliet, 2005).

In addition, there is a lack of studies involving the relationship between forgiveness, compassion, and interdependent happiness as previous studies belong mostly to American and Western societies that have confined their efforts only to individual-focused happiness. Indian society is said to be a society having a collectivistic culture, so studying interdependent happiness will be more relevant to explicate the couple relationship. In this backdrop of the facts and arguments, the presents study has been planned to underscore the impacts of intrapersonal and interpersonal dimensions of forgiveness and compassion in shaping hedonic, social, psychological and social well-being as well as interdependent happiness of married couples.

The scientific study of forgiveness and compassion has great relevance to understanding the nature and dynamics of intrapersonal, interpersonal, community and organizational relationships due to their universality, unavoidability and positive outcomes associated with the practice of these constructs. The findings of the study may be applied to unearth the antecedents and correlates of forgiveness and compassion to assess their role in causing hedonic and eudaimonic well-being. The findings of the study may certainly be useful to understand the causes of well-being in other close interpersonal relationships, to develop interventions to explicate and solve couple and family problems, and other situations of interpersonal nature. The findings may also be useful for various organizations such as police, jail, government organizations and other organizations. In this backdrop, the present study aims to study the nature of relationships among compassion for others, self-compassion, forgiveness, well-being and interdependent happiness of Hindu married couples.

3.2 Objectives

The following objectives were identified for the present study:

1. To explicate the nature and extent of relationships among compassion for others, self-compassion, well-being and interdependent happiness of Hindu married couples,

2. To understand the nature and extent of the relationship among forgiveness, well-being and interdependent happiness of Hindu married couples,

3. To estimate the variance accounted for by compassion for others and self-compassion in the scores of interdependent happiness of Hindu married couples,

4. To estimate the variance accounted for by compassion for others and self-compassion in the scores of the well-being of Hindu married couples,

5. To estimate the variance accounted for by forgiveness in the scores of interdependent happiness of Hindu married couples, and

6. To estimate the variance accounted for by forgiveness in the scores of the well-being of Hindu married couples.

3.3 Hypotheses

The following hypotheses have been framed for the current study:

1. There will be positive correlations among compassion for others, self-compassion, well-being and interdependent happiness of Hindu married couples.

2. There will be positive correlations among forgiveness, well-being and interdependent happiness of Hindu married couples.

3. Compassion (compassion for others and self-compassion) will cause significant variability in interdependent happiness of Hindu married couples.

4. Compassion (compassion for others and self-compassion) will also lead to significant variability in the well-being of Hindu married couples.

5. Forgiveness will account for significant variance in the scores of interdependent happiness of Hindu married couples.

6. Forgiveness will account for significant variance in the scores of the well-being of Hindu married couples.

3.4 Methods and Procedure

3.4.1 Sample

The study employed a correlational research design in which a snowball sampling technique was used to choose the participants. The data were collected from married Hindu couples (n = 600, *Age Range* = 26-56 years, *Mean Age* = 38.42 years, *SD* = 7.89) who were the residents of Sagar city, Madhya Pradesh, India. Most of the participants were chosen from the middle-class Hindu families. The biographic details such as education, gender, age, length of the marriage and nature of family were recorded with the help of a questionnaire. A family is a group of individuals related by marriage, birth, consanguinity or legal adoption who share a common kitchen and financial resources regularly. A nuclear family is defined by a single married couple with or without their unmarried children whereas joint family is collection two or more married couples (horizontal level) or three or more married couples (vertical level) of a single generation with their married or unmarried children (Sharma, 2013).

3.4.2 Inclusion and Exclusion Criteria

The participants with the age ranging between 25 to 60 years with at least five years of married life and the apparent normal physical and mental health (as reported by the participants) were chosen for the study. The participant with a minimum of five years of married life was chosen as a criterion so that he/she may have acquired sufficient experience of the basic issues and dynamics of married life. Only Hindu married couples were included in the study as Hindu marriage is a sacrament rather than a contract. Those couples who belonged to other religious communities, having some health problems, had lived less than five years of married life and did not fell under the prescribed age range were excluded from the study. Unhealthy participants were excluded to avoid any confounding impacts of health-related distress on happiness (Angner et al., 2009, 2013; Steptoe, 2019).

3.4.3 Tools

The current study employed five scales which were originally available in the English language. As the chosen sample was Hindi-speaking, the scales were translated in the Hindi language. According to accepted procedure by the earlier researchers, the scales of the study were translated in Hindi from English and again from English to Hindi by a team of three experts (Behr, 2017; Brislin, 1970). These experts also ascertained the face validity and validated each item of the scales keeping in mind the conceptualization of the constructs. The present study employed the following tools for data collection:

3.4.3.1 Compassion for Others Scale

The scale was developed by Pommier (2011). It consists of 24 items (e.g., When people cry in front of me I usually don't feel anything at all), and is subdivided into 6 subscales; (1) kindness, (2) indifference, (3) common humanity, (4) separation, (5) mindfulness, and (6) disengagement. Participants respond to items on a 1-5 Likert scale (1 = *almost never* & 5 = *almost always*), with indifference, separation, and disengagement items reverse-scored. Cronbach alpha's for overall scale = 0.9, with kindness = 0.77, indifference = 0.68, common humanity 0.7, separation 0.64, mindfulness = 0.67, and disengagement 0.57. Content, convergent and discriminant validity of the Compassion for Others Scale is supported in USA populations (Pommier, 2011).

3.4.3.2 Self-Compassion Scale

Self-compassion Scale (SCS) standardized and developed by (Neff, 2003b) was employed to assess the levels of self-compassion of the married Hindu couples. This measure entails the emotions, behaviours and thoughts of individuals which originate during the odds of human life. In other words, the scale purports to measure the occurrence of feelings and thoughts of suffering, pain and inadequacy, and deal these experiences with the psychological mechanisms which may involve the dynamics of self-kindness, common humanity, mindfulness, isolation, over-identification and self-judgment. The measure comprises of a set of 26 items related to these six components of self-compassion which are assessed on a five-point scale ranging from almost never to almost always.

The items on self-kindness (5, 12, 19, 23, 26), common humanity (3, 7, 10, 15) and mindfulness (9, 14, 17, 22) subscales are assigned 1, 2, 3, 4 and 5 scores for the responses ranging from *almost never* to *almost always*. The reverse scoring was done for the responses on self-judgment (1, 8, 11, 16, 21), isolation (4, 13, 18, 25) and over-identification (2, 6, 20, 24) subscales. An aggregate of the scores on these subscales was indicated the score of the participants on self-compassion scale. For SCS, higher scores indicate higher self-compassion. The reliability and validity of the scale have been well established in many studies (Neff et al., 2017; Pandey et al., 2019). The Cronbach's Alpha of the SCS scale for the current sample was .571.

3.4.3.3 Heartland Forgiveness Scale

Heartland Forgiveness Scale (HFS) was developed by Thompson et al. (2005) to measure one's forgiveness level with 18 items. HFS is a 7-point Likert-type scale which span from "*almost always false than true*" (1) to "*almost always true of me*" (7) HFS has three subscales; forgiveness of others, forgiveness of situation and forgiveness of self. Higher scores on each subscale reflect a higher level of forgiveness in each domain. The HFS has been reported to have adequate psychometric properties in previous studies (Thompson et al., 2005). Cronbach alpha (internal consistency) coefficients for the forgiveness of self, others, situations and overall Heartland Forgiveness Scale were found .75, .78, and .77 and .86, respectively (Thompson et al., 2005).

3.4.3.4 Interdependent Happiness Scale

The Interdependent Happiness Scale (IHS) developed by Hitokoto and Uchida (2015) was employed to measure the interdependent happiness of the couples. This measure assesses the happiness of individuals which is derived and maintained from their experiences arising out of ordinariness, quiescence and interpersonal harmony. It consists of 9 items (e. g., I believe that I and those around me are happy.) with a five-point scale (1-*Strongly disagree*, 2-*Somewhat disagree*, 3-*Neither agree nor disagree*, 4-*Somewhat agree*, 5-*Strongly agree*). A total sum of the scores on all items of the scale shows the interdependent happiness of the participants. Higher scores on IHS signify higher levels of interdependent happiness. The psychometric properties of interdependent happiness scale were found to be technically satisfactory in a set of earlier studies conducted on samples chosen from diverse populations (Markus & Kitayama, 1991; Oishi et al., 1999; Suh & Oishi, 2004; Uchida & Ogihara, 2012; Uchida & Kitayama, 2009). Hitokoto and Uchida (2015) reported desirable levels of internal consistency across cultures (Germany: $\alpha = .60$; Japan: $\alpha = .78$; Korea: $\alpha = .78$; US: $\alpha = .61$). The Cronbach's Alpha of the IHS for the present sample of the study was .756.

3.4.3.5 Mental Health Continuum-Short Form

For assessing the hedonic and eudaimonic well-being of the participants, the mental health continuum-short form (MHC-SF) was used. The scale was developed by Keyes (2005). The scale was developed on three theoretical sources. These sources are the findings of emotional well-being (Diener et al., 1999), eudaimonic well-being (Ryff, 1989), hedonic well-being and social well being (Keyes, 1998). This measure of well-being comprises of 14 items and the participants rate their experiences on a 6-point scale which ranges from *never, once or twice, about once a week, 2 or 3 times a week, almost every day,* to *every day* during the last month. Emotional well-being, psychological well-being and social well being are measured through 3, 6 and 5 items, respectively. The internal consistency reliability is >.80 (Keyes, 2005).

3.4.4 Procedure

The research proposal was prepared and submitted to the Ethics Committee constituted by Doctor Harisingh Gour Vishwavidyalaya, Sagar, 470003, Madhya Pradesh, India for approval and conduct the study. The participants were chosen as per the inclusion and exclusion criteria after the collection of their written consent. The questionnaires were procured and the sample was chosen which followed the data collection process. All relevant demographic details about this study were taken from the participants like education, age, gender, nature of family and length of married life. Before conducting the actual data collection, the precautions and instructions was read and understood. Six hundred fifty sets of all the questionnaires were prepared for administration. The guidelines of scoring given in the manuals of each scale were consulted for awarding scores to the responses of the participants.

3.4.5 Data Analysis Plan

According to the research questions, the mean scores, standard deviations (SDs), coefficient of correlation and hierarchical regression analysis were computed. The obtained raw scores were arranged as per the nature of statistical techniques. The statistical analyses were carried out with the help of SPSS 26v procured by the University. The data was screened before analysis for removing the genuine outliers. As the data did not show normal distribution, the bootstrapping method employing 1000 samples was used to compute various statistics. Education (1= non-graduate, 2 = graduate), gender (1= male, 2 = female) and nature of family (1= nuclear, 2 = joint) were categorical variables while age, years of marriage, compassion for others, self-compassion, forgiveness, interdependent happiness and well-being were continuous measures. The demographic attributes, compassion for others, self-compassion and forgiveness measures were the predictors whereas interdependent happiness and well-being were the criterion measures.

CHAPTER - 4
RESULTS

RESULTS

The basic objectives of the current study were to understand the nature and degree of the relationships among compassion for others, self-compassion, forgiveness, flourishing and interdependent happiness and to estimate the variance accounted for by compassion for others, self-compassion and forgiveness in the scores of flourishing and interdependent happiness of Hindu married couples. To achieve the first objective, the coefficient of correlations among all the predictors and criterion measures were computed. Further, hierarchical regression analysis was carried out to understand the variability accounted for by education, gender, age, years of marriage, compassion for others, self-compassion and forgiveness in the scores of flourishing and interdependent happiness of the participants. Before carrying out statistical analysis, the data were screened for identifying outliers and inadvertent entries by running frequency and anomaly index in SPSS 26v. As the data were not normally distributed, the bootstrapping method of computing correlations and hierarchical regression were employed adopting the criteria of 1000 bootstrap samples.

For the purpose of reference, the mean scores and standard deviation (SD) of age, years of marriage, compassion for others (kindness, indifference, common humanity, separation, mindfulness, and disengagement) self-kindness, self-judgement, common humanity, isolation, mindfulness, over-identification, self-compassion, forgiveness of self, forgiveness of others, forgiveness of situation, overall forgiveness, interdependent happiness, hedonic well-being, eudaimonic well-being and human flourishing (well-being) of the male, female and all the participants in terms of their levels of education (non-graduate, graduate) and nature of family (nuclear, joint) have been presented in Table 4.1. The results of the study have been presented in two sections. In the first section, coefficients of the correlations among all the predictors and criterion measures have been presented followed by regression analysis which is presented in section two.

Table 4.1
Mean scores and SDs of the measures (N= 600)

Measures	Non-graduate								Graduate							
	Male				Female				Male				Female			
	Nuclear (n =87)		Joint (n = 134)		Nuclear (n = 81)		Joint (n = 120)		Nuclear (n = 23)		Joint (n = 56)		Nuclear (n = 26)		Joint (n = 73)	
	Mean	SD	Mean	SD	Mean	SD	Mean	SD	Mean	SD	Mean	SD	Mean	SD	Mean	SD
Age (in years)	41.26	6.95	39.87	7.74	38.06	8.09	35.03	7.01	40.7	7.83	38.5	7.49	37.39	8.79	37.89	8.46
Years of Marriage	15.76	7.90	15.01	7.81	15.44	7.48	12.64	6.57	17.52	7.95	14.29	7.89	17.35	8.78	17.92	8.32
Kindness	13.24	3.36	13.50	3.10	13.36	3.51	12.86	3.25	11.74	2.58	12.36	3.22	11.96	2.44	12.67	2.93
indifference	13.61	3.18	14.46	3.10	13.41	3.52	13.99	3.30	14.30	2.60	13.00	3.19	12.50	3.47	13.22	3.35
Common Humanity	13.68	2.80	13.87	2.66	13.32	3.12	14.05	2.76	14.09	2.94	12.89	2.61	13.73	2.75	12.55	2.88
Separation	13.52	2.98	14.10	2.88	13.99	3.11	13.89	3.07	13.87	2.7	13.27	2.90	12.19	2.47	13.25	2.79
Mindfulness	13.32	2.72	13.40	2.76	13.38	2.78	12.71	3.08	11.78	3.27	12.11	3.08	13.35	2.68	12.37	2.41
Disengagement	13.90	3.14	14.55	3.46	14.67	3.63	14.45	3.26	14.87	3.35	12.89	3.21	13.62	3.40	13.96	3.05
Compassion for Others	148.63	18.37	153.22	21.44	149.58	20.67	149.45	23.50	146.43	18.49	140.14	17.47	141.08	17.09	142.07	20.01
Self-kindness	17.55	4.01	16.71	3.51	15.15	4.16	16.39	3.99	17.13	3.81	15.38	3.56	16.65	3.83	15.63	3.59
Self-judgement	13.75	3.78	15.78	3.87	15.67	3.74	15.75	3.89	15.74	3.93	15.63	3.80	14.69	3.61	15.11	3.62
Common Humanity	14.30	3.38	14.13	3.90	12.95	3.43	13.58	4.08	14.74	2.92	12.63	3.36	13.27	3.41	13.00	3.21
Isolation	11.54	3.82	11.96	3.66	12.38	3.72	13.15	3.86	10.35	2.99	12.79	2.83	11.92	3.05	12.29	2.74
Mindfulness	14.22	3.05	14.03	3.53	13.44	3.16	13.3	4.22	12.13	2.62	12.95	3.72	12.96	2.41	12.16	3.33
Over-identification	11.68	3.45	12.47	3.78	12.16	3.57	12.88	3.70	10.74	4.00	12.48	2.70	10.65	2.65	12.38	3.38
Self-compassion	154.39	17.07	157.70	24.76	151.34	18.64	157.23	24.77	150.91	11.39	151.19	16.95	149.65	15.07	148.77	17.70
Forgiveness of self	25.66	4.27	25.67	4.18	26.71	4.35	26.05	4.00	24.78	4.09	25.07	3.34	25.15	3.92	24.08	3.98
Forgiveness of others	26.07	5.06	26.89	5.55	27.27	5.98	26.82	6.02	26.13	3.36	24.32	4.87	26.04	4.78	26.00	5.00
Forgiveness of situation	25.92	3.36	26.03	4.478	25.69	4.19	25.52	4.74	25.13	2.75	24.41	3.49	25.12	4.24	24.88	3.68
Overall Forgiveness	129.37	15.77	131.15	18.46	133.67	20.16	131.25	18.75	126.96	11.05	123.20	14.11	127.50	17.208	125.04	16.47
Interdependent Happiness	33.60	6.51	32.49	6.308	34.06	5.87	31.63	7.74	33.65	4.50	32.18	7.24	32.62	6.97	31.29	5.55
Hedonic Well-being	11.80	3.05	10.95	3.55	11.35	3.54	10.44	4.17	11.61	3.03	10.63	4.08	9.69	4.48	9.82	4.097
Eudaimonic Well-being	40.61	8.37	36.07	9.57	38.91	9.06	36.20	9.97	31.43	10.25	33.46	9.41	33.58	10.87	32.37	9.72
Human Flourishing	52.40	10.70	47.02	12.01	50.26	11.21	46.64	12.87	43.04	12.02	44.09	12.26	43.27	14.45	42.19	12.78

4.1 SECTION ONE: CORRELATION ANALYSIS

4.1.1 Coefficients of Correlation for the Male Participants

The Pearson Product Moment coefficients of correlation among the continuous demographic characteristics (such as age and years of marriage), kindness, indifference, common humanity, separation, mindfulness, disengagement, compassion for others, self-kindness, self-judgement, common humanity, isolation, mindfulness, over-identification, self-compassion, forgiveness of self, forgiveness of others, forgiveness of situation, overall forgiveness, interdependent happiness, hedonic well-being, eudaimonic well-being and human flourishing of the males, females and entire participants were computed. The coefficients of correlation of the male participants have been displayed in Table 4.2.

Age was positively correlated with hedonic well-being ($r = .22$, $p = .01$) and human flourishing ($r = .15$, $p = .01$) of male participants. Years of marriage showed significant positive correlations with forgiveness of others ($r = .23$, $p = .01$) and overall forgiveness ($r = .15$, $p = .01$), hedonic well-being ($r = .17$, $p = .01$) of male participants (see Table 4.2).

Kindness was positively correlated with interdependent happiness ($r = .27$, $p = .01$), hedonic well-being ($r = .23$, $p = .01$), eudaimonic well-being ($r = .29$, $p = .01$) and human flourishing ($r = .30$, $p = .01$) of the male participants. Common humanity was positively correlated with interdependent happiness ($r = .27$, $p = .01$), hedonic well-being ($r = .21$, $p = .01$), eudaimonic well-being ($r = .27$, $p = .01$) and human flourishing ($r = .28$, $p = .01$) of the male participants. Mindfulness was positively correlated with interdependent happiness ($r = .27$, $p = .01$), hedonic well-being ($r = .23$, $p = .01$), eudaimonic well-being ($r = .22$, $p = .01$) and human flourishing (**$r = .22$, $p = .01$**) of male participants (see Table 4.2).

Disengagement was positively correlated with hedonic well-being ($r = .12$, $p = .05$), eudaimonic well-being ($r = .12$, $p = .05$) and human flourishing ($r = .13$, $p = .05$) of male participants. Overall compassion for others was positively correlated with interdependent happiness ($r = .27$, $p = .01$), hedonic well-being ($r = .24$, $p = .01$), eudaimonic well-being ($r = .28$, $p = .01$) and human flourishing ($r = .30$, $p = .01$) of male participants (see Table 4.2).

Self-kindness was positively correlated with interdependent happiness ($r = .36$, $p = .01$), hedonic well-being ($r = .37$, $p = .01$), eudaimonic well-being ($r = .33$, $p = .01$) and human flourishing ($r = .37$, $p = .01$) of male participants. Self-judgement showed significant negative correlations with interdependent happiness ($r = .11$, $p = .05$), eudaimonic well-being ($r = .13$, $p = .01$) and human flourishing ($r = .12$, $p = .01$) of male participants. Common humanity had significant positive correlations with interdependent happiness ($r = .34$, $p = .01$), hedonic well-being ($r = .27$, $p = .01$), eudaimonic well-being ($r = .29$, $p = .01$) and human flourishing ($r = .31$, $p = .01$) of male participants (see Table 4.2).

Mindfulness exhibited positive correlations with interdependent happiness ($r = .30$, $p = .01$), hedonic well-being ($r = .15$, $p = .05$), eudaimonic well-being ($r = .25$, $p = .01$) and human flourishing ($r = .24$, $p = .01$) of male participants. Overall self-compassion showed significant positive correlations with interdependent happiness ($r = .24$, $p = .01$), hedonic well-being ($r = .26$, $p = .01$), eudaimonic well-being ($r = .26$, $p = .01$) and human flourishing ($r = .29$, $p = .01$) of male participants. Forgiveness of self showed significant positive correlations with hedonic well-being ($r = .15$, $p = .01$), eudaimonic well-being ($r = .13$, $p = .05$) and human flourishing ($r = .15$, $p = .05$) of male participants. Forgiveness of others showed significant positive correlations with hedonic well-being ($r = .16$, $p = .01$), eudaimonic well-being ($r = .16$, $p = .01$) and human flourishing ($r = .17$, $p = .01$) of male participants (see Table 4.2).

Table 4.2

Correlations Among Predictors and Criterion Measures of the Male Participants (n = 300)

Measures	Age	YOM	KIN	IND	CoH	SEP	MIN	DIS	CFO	SK	SJ	CH	I	M	OI	SCS	FS	FO	FOS	HFS	IDH	HWB	EWB	HF
Age	1																							
YOM	.86**	1																						
KIN	.30*	.06	1																					
IND	.18**	.16**	.04	1																				
CoH	.13*	.09	.45**	.06	1																			
SEP	.16**	.14*	.04	.52**	.04	1																		
MIN	.07	.04	.56**	.04	.39**	.01	1																	
DIS	.22**	.21**	.14*	.63**	.11	.56**	.20**	1																
CFO	.24**	.18**	.65**	.61**	.57**	.56**	.62**	.66**	1															
SK	.19**	.16**	.36**	.11	.26**	.10	.36**	.19**	.38**	1														
SJ	-.06	-.035	-.09	.35**	-.08	.28**	-.05	.21**	.16**	-.07	1													
CH	.11*	.10	.38**	.18**	.41**	.16**	.32**	.32**	.48**	.41**	-.13*	1												
I	.03	-.06	-.11*	.19**	-.05	.18**	.08	.13*	.10	-.18**	.36**	-.12*	1											
M	.15*	.11	.41**	.17**	.31**	.13*	.44**	.23**	.47	.42**	-.10	.48**	.04	1										
OI	.15**	.08	-.05	.30**	-.21**	.26**	-.12*	.21**	.09	-.05	.36**	-.12*	.46**	-.10	1									
SCS	.17**	.11	.32**	.41**	.25**	.35**	.38**	.24**	.58**	.55**	.47**	.55**	.47**	.62**	.37**	1								
FS	.08	.06	.13*	.08	.01	.08	.09	.09	.13*	.05	.11	.13*	.09	.14*	.15**	.21**	1							
FO	.22**	.23**	.23**	.27**	.19**	.18**	.20**	.39**	.38**	.29**	.18**	.24**	.04	.22**	.15**	.37**	.25**	1						
FOS	.13*	.05	.24**	.21**	.30**	.20**	.26**	.29**	.40**	.23**	.13*	.23**	.16**	.31**	.17**	.40**	.27**	.34**	1					
HFS	.21**	.19**	.27**	.26**	.19**	.20**	.23**	.36**	.40**	.26**	.19**	.13*	.11	.28**	.21**	.43**	.71**	.83**	.58**	1				
IDH	.10	.11	.27**	.06	.27**	.01	.27**	.04	.27**	.36**	-.11*	.34**	-.18**	.30**	-.07	.24**	.11	.07	.16**	.13*	1			
HWB	.22**	.17**	.23**	.04	.21**	.04	.23**	.12*	.24**	.37**	-.06	.27**	-.03	.15*	.11	.26**	.15**	.16**	.14*	.21**	.37**	1		
EWB	.11	.01	.29**	.04	.27**	.07	.22**	.12*	.28**	.33**	-.13*	.29**	-.01	.25**	.07	.26**	.13*	.16**	.27**	.22**	.33**	.59**	1	
HF	.15*	.06	.30**	.04	.28**	.06	.24**	.13*	.30**	.37**	-.12*	.31**	-.01	.24**	.09	.29**	.15*	.17**	.26**	.24**	.37**	.77**	.97**	1

Note 1: YOM = Years of Marriage, KIN = Kindness, IND = Indifference, CoH = Common Humanity, SEP = Separation, MIN = Mindfulness, DIS = Disengagement, CFO = Compassion for Others, SK = Self-Kindness, SJ = Self-Judgment, CH = Common Humanity, I = Isolation, M = Mindfulness, OI = Over-Identification, SCS = Self-Compassion Scale, FS = Forgiveness of self, FO = Forgiveness of others, FOS = Forgiveness of situation, HFS = Heartland Forgiveness Scale, IDH = Interdependent Happiness, HWB = Hedonic Well-being, EWB = Eudaimonic Well-being and HF = Human Flourishing

Note 2: * . Correlation is significant at the .05 level, **. Correlation is significant at the .01 level

Forgiveness of situation showed significant positive correlations with interdependent happiness ($r = .16$, $p = .01$), hedonic well-being ($r = .14$, $p = .05$), eudaimonic well-being ($r = .27$, $p = .01$) and human flourishing ($r = .26$, $p = .01$) of male participants. Overall forgiveness showed significant positive correlations with interdependent happiness ($r = .13$, $p = .05$), hedonic well-being ($r = .21$, $p = .01$), eudaimonic well-being ($r = .22$, $p = .01$) and human flourishing ($r = .24$, $p = .01$) of male participants (see Table 4.2).

4.1.2 Coefficients of Correlation for the Female Participants

The coefficients of correlation among the predictors and criterion measures of the female participants have been displayed in Table 4.3. Age showed significant positive correlations with interdependent happiness ($r = .13$, $p = .05$), hedonic well-being ($r = .20$, $p = .01$), eudaimonic well-being ($r = .18$, $p = .01$) and human flourishing ($r = .20$, $p = .01$) of female participants. Years of marriage showed significant positive correlations with hedonic well-being ($r = .21$, $p = .01$), eudaimonic well-being ($r = .12$, $p = .05$) and human flourishing ($r = .16$, $p = .01$) of female participants. Kindness showed significant positive correlations with interdependent happiness ($r = .26$, $p = .01$), hedonic well-being ($r = .24$, $p = .01$), eudaimonic well-being ($r = .38$, $p = .01$) and human flourishing ($r = .37$, $p = .01$) of female participants. Indifference showed significant positive correlations with hedonic well-being ($r = .23$, $p = .01$), eudaimonic well-being ($r = .18$, $p = .01$) and human flourishing ($r = .21$, $p = .01$) of female participants (see Table 4.3).

Table 4.3

Correlations among predictors and criterion measures of the female participants (n = 300)

Measures	Age	YOM	KIN	IND	CoH	SEP	MIN	DIS	CFO	SK	SJ	CH	I	M	OI	SCS	FS	FO	FOS	HFS	IDH	HWB	EWB	HF
Age	1																							
YOM	.82**	1																						
KIN	.21**	.16**	1																					
IND	.23**	.30**	.20**	1																				
CoH	.23**	.14*	.48**	.20**	1																			
SEP	.10	.14*	.12*	.53**	.11	1																		
MIN	.13*	.10	.42**	.13*	.33**	.03	1																	
DIS	.20**	.24**	.23**	.62**	.19**	.58**	.16**	1																
CFO	.29**	.26**	.67**	.70**	.62**	.60**	.55**	.67**	1															
SK	-.01	-.06	.29**	.10	.25**	.06	.21**	.12*	.28**	1														
SJ	-.04	-.01	-.08	.13*	-.01	.18**	.03	.12*	.09	-.12*	1													
CH	.13*	.07	.32**	.12*	.31**	.08	.34**	.15**	.35**	.39**	-.20**	1												
I	-.05	-.10	-.06	.19**	-.06	.26**	-.05	.19**	.11	-.15*	.31**	.01	1											
M	.17**	.08	.28**	.24**	.29**	.24**	.33**	.19**	.37**	.44**	-.10	.48**	.10	1										
OI	.01	.06	-.05	.17**	-.06	.06	-.03	.22**	.12*	-.13*	.35**	-.08	.43**	.05	1									
SCS	.07	.06	.26**	.30**	.26**	.26**	.30**	.31**	.44**	.55**	.37**	.58**	.50**	.68**	.38**	1								
FS	-.02	-.07	.19**	.12*	.19**	.07	.22**	.14*	.24**	.16**	.01	.17**	.05	.20**	.10	.22**	1							
FO	.17**	.20**	.30**	.25**	.34**	.22**	.30**	.30**	.45**	.24**	.15*	.23**	.13*	.25**	.19**	.38**	.35**	1						
FOS	.17**	.16**	.31**	.19**	.30**	.14*	.32**	.23**	.39**	.24**	.21**	.15**	.22**	.30**	.22**	.43**	.31**	.45**	1					
HFS	.13*	.12*	.34**	.25**	.36**	.20**	.36**	.30**	.47**	.27**	.14*	.25**	.15**	.31**	.21**	.43**	.73**	.87**	.64**	1				
IDH	.13*	.10	.26**	-.03	.28**	-.09	.29**	.06	.20**	.24**	-.14*	.33**	-.09	.25**	-.04	.20**	.15**	.18**	.14*	.21**	1			
HWB	.20**	.21**	.24**	.23**	.33**	.22**	.31**	.26**	.42**	.24**	-.06	.28**	.07	.25**	.03	.28**	.13*	.26**	.28**	.28**	.48**	1		
EWB	.18**	.12*	.38**	.18**	.26**	.16**	.30**	.17**	.39**	.29**	-.05	.22**	.06	.24**	-.07	.26**	.20**	.31**	.26**	.34**	.45**	.61**	1	
HF	.20**	.16**	.37**	.21**	.31**	.20**	.33**	.21**	.43**	.30**	-.06	.26**	.07	.27**	-.05	.29**	.20**	.33**	.29**	.35**	.50**	.79**	.97**	1

Note 1: YOM = Years of Marriage, KIN = Kindness, IND = Indifference, CoH = Common Humanity, SEP = Separation, MIN = Mindfulness, DIS = Disengagement, CFO = Compassion for Others, SK = Self-Kindness, SJ = Self-Judgment, CH = Common Humanity, I = Isolation, M = Mindfulness, OI = Over-Identification, SCS = Self-Compassion Scale, FS = Forgiveness of self, FO = Forgiveness of others, FOS = Forgiveness of situation, HFS = Heartland Forgiveness Scale, IDH = Interdependent Happiness, HWB = Hedonic Well-being, EWB = Eudaimonic Well-being and HF = Human Flourishing

Note 2: *. Correlation is significant at the .05 level, **. Correlation is significant at the .01 level

Common humanity showed significant positive correlations with interdependent happiness ($r = .28$, $p = .01$), hedonic well-being ($r = .33$, $p = .01$), eudaimonic well-being ($r = .26$, $p = .01$) and human flourishing ($r = .31$, $p = .01$) of female participants. Separation showed significant positive correlations with hedonic well-being ($r = .22$, $p = .01$), eudaimonic well-being ($r = .16$, $p = .01$) and human flourishing ($r = .20$, $p = .01$) of female participants. Mindfulness showed significant positive correlations with interdependent happiness ($r = .29$, $p = .01$), hedonic well-being ($r = .31$, $p = .01$), eudaimonic well-being ($r = .30$, $p = .01$) and human flourishing ($r = .33$, $p = .01$) of female participants (see Table 4.3).

Disengagement showed significant positive correlations with hedonic well-being ($r = .26$, $p = .01$), eudaimonic well-being ($r = .17$, $p = .01$) and human flourishing ($r = .21$, $p = .01$) of female participants. Overall compassion for others showed significant positive correlations with interdependent happiness ($r = .20$, $p = .01$), hedonic well-being ($r = .42$, $p = .01$), eudaimonic well-being ($r = .39$, $p = .01$) and human flourishing ($r = .43$, $p = .01$) of female participants. Self-kindness showed significant positive correlations with interdependent happiness ($r = .24$, $p = .01$), hedonic well-being ($r = .34$, $p = .01$), eudaimonic well-being ($r = .29$, $p = .01$) and human flourishing ($r = .30$, $p = .01$) of female participants. Self-kindness showed significant negative correlations with the scores of self-judgement ($r = .12$, $p = .05$), isolation ($r = .15$, $p = .05$) and over-identification ($r = .13$, $p = .05$) of female participants (see Table 4.3).

Self-judgement showed significant positive correlation with interdependent happiness ($r = .14$, $p = .05$) of female participants. Common humanity showed significant positive correlations with interdependent happiness ($r = .33$, $p = .01$), hedonic well-being ($r = .28$, $p = .01$), eudaimonic well-being ($r = .22$, $p = .01$) and human flourishing ($r = .26$, $p = .01$) of female participants. Common humanity showed significant negative correlations only with the scores of self-judgement ($r = .20$, $p = .01$) of female participants (see Table 4.3).

Mindfulness showed significant positive correlations with interdependent happiness ($r = .25$, $p = .01$), hedonic well-being ($r = .25$, $p = .01$), eudaimonic well-being ($r = .24$, $p = .01$) and human flourishing ($r = .27$, $p = .01$) of female participants. Overall self-compassion showed significant positive correlations with interdependent happiness ($r = .20$, $p = .01$), hedonic well-being ($r = .28$, $p = .01$), eudaimonic well-being ($r = .26$, $p = .01$) and human flourishing ($r = .29$, $p = .01$) of female participants. Forgiveness of self showed significant positive correlations with interdependent happiness ($r = .15$, $p = .01$), hedonic well-being ($r = .13$, $p = .05$), eudaimonic well-being ($r = .20$, $p = .01$) and human flourishing ($r = .20$, $p = .01$) of female participants (see Table 4.3).

Forgiveness of others showed significant positive correlations with interdependent happiness ($r = .18$, $p = .01$), hedonic well-being ($r = .26$, $p = .01$), eudaimonic well-being ($r = .31$, $p = .01$) and human flourishing ($r = .33$, $p = .01$) of female participants. Forgiveness of situation showed significant positive correlations with interdependent happiness ($r = .14$, $p = .05$), hedonic well-being ($r = .28$, $p = .01$), eudaimonic well-being ($r = .26$, $p = .01$) and human flourishing ($r = .29$, $p = .01$) of female participants. Overall forgiveness showed significant positive correlations with interdependent happiness ($r = .21$, $p = .01$), hedonic well-being ($r = .28$, $p = .01$), eudaimonic well-being ($r = .34$, $p = .01$) and human flourishing ($r = .35$, $p = .01$) of female participants (see Table 4.3).

4.1.3 Coefficients of Correlation for All the Participants

The coefficients of correlation among the predictors and criterion measures of the all participants have been displayed in Table 4.4. Age showed significant positive correlations with interdependent happiness ($r = .12$, $p = .01$), hedonic well-being ($r = .22$, $p = .01$), eudaimonic well-being ($r = .15$, $p = .01$) and human flourishing ($r = .18$, $p = .01$) of all the participants (see Table 4.4).

Years of marriage showed significant positive correlations with interdependent happiness ($r = .11$, $p = .05$), hedonic well-being ($r = .19$, $p = .01$) and human flourishing ($r = .11$, $p = .01$) of all the participants. Kindness showed significant positive correlations with interdependent happiness ($r = .27$, $p = .01$), hedonic well-being ($r = .24$, $p = .01$), eudaimonic well-being ($r = .34$, $p = .01$) and human flourishing ($r = .34$, $p = .01$) of all the participants. Kindness showed significant negative correlations with the scores of self-judgement ($r = .09$, $p = .05$) and isolation ($r = .09$, $p = .05$) of all the participants (see Table 4.4).

Indifference showed significant positive correlations with hedonic well-being ($r = .15$, $p = .01$), eudaimonic well-being ($r = .12$, $p = .01$) and human flourishing ($r = .14$, $p = .01$) of all the participants. Common humanity showed significant positive correlations with interdependent happiness ($r = .28$, $p = .01$), hedonic well-being ($r = .28$, $p = .01$), eudaimonic well-being ($r = .27$, $p = .01$) and human flourishing ($r = .30$, $p = .01$) of all the participants. Common humanity showed significant negative correlations only with the scores of over-identification ($r = .13$, $p = .01$) of all the participants. Separation showed significant positive correlations with hedonic well-being ($r = .14$, $p = .01$), eudaimonic well-being ($r = .12$, $p = .01$) and human flourishing ($r = .13$, $p = .01$) of all the participants. Mindfulness showed significant positive correlations with interdependent happiness ($r = .28$, $p = .01$), hedonic well-being ($r = .28$, $p = .01$), eudaimonic well-being ($r = .26$, $p = .01$) and human flourishing ($r = .29$, $p = .01$) of all the participants (see Table 4.4).

Table 4.4

Correlations among predictors and criterion measures of all the participants (N = 600)

Measures	Age	YOM	KIN	IND	CoH	SEP	MIN	DIS	CFO	SK	SJ	CH	I	M	OI	SCS	FS	FO	FOS	HFS	IDH	HWB	EWB	HF
Age	1																							
YOM	.82**	1																						
KIN	.17**	.11**	1																					
IND	.21**	.20**	.12**	1																				
CoH	.19**	.12**	.47**	.14**	1																			
SEP	.13**	.14**	.08*	.52**	.06	1																		
MIN	.10*	.07	.50**	.09*	.36**	.02	1																	
DIS	.20**	.22**	.19**	.62**	.15**	.57**	.18**	1																
CFO	.27**	.22**	.66**	.60**	.58**	.58**	.28**	.66**	1															
SK	.10*	.05	.33**	.11**	.26**	.08*	.28**	.15**	.33**	1														
SJ	-.06	-.01	-.09*	.24**	-.05	.23**	-.01	.17**	.12**	-.10*	1													
CH	.14**	.09*	.35**	.16**	.36**	.12**	.33**	.23**	.42**	.41**	-.16**	1												
I	-.03	-.05	-.09*	.18**	-.06	.21**	.01	.17**	.10*	-.17**	.34**	-.07	1											
M	.18**	.10*	.34**	.22**	.30**	.10*	.39**	.20**	.42**	.44**	-.10*	.49**	.06	1										
OI	.07	.07	.23**	.36**	-.13**	.25**	-.08	.22**	.10*	-.09*	.36**	-.11**	.44**	-.02	1									
SCS	.13**	.07	.29**	.36**	.26**	.30**	.34**	.36**	.51**	.55**	.42**	.57**	.47**	.65**	.37**	1								
FS	.02	-.00	.16**	.10*	.10*	.08	.15**	.12**	.19**	.10*	.06	.15**	.07	.17**	.13**	.21**	1							
FO	.18**	.21**	.26**	.27**	.27**	.20**	.25**	.35**	.41**	.26**	.17**	.23**	.09*	.23**	.17**	.37**	.31**	1						
FOS	.15**	.10*	.28**	.20**	.30**	.17**	.29**	.26**	.40**	.23**	.17**	.19**	.18**	.31**	.19**	.41**	.29**	.39**	1					
HFS	.15**	.15**	.30**	.25**	.28**	.20**	.29**	.33**	.43**	.26**	.17**	.25**	.13**	.29**	.21**	.43**	.72**	.85**	.61**	1				
IDH	.12**	.10*	.27**	.02	.28**	-.04	.28**	.05	.23**	.30**	-.13**	.34**	-.14**	.28**	-.06	.22**	.13**	.12**	.15**	.17**	1			
HWB	.22**	.19**	.24**	.20**	.28**	.14**	.28**	.19**	.34**	.34**	-.07	.28**	.02	.21**	-.06	.28**	.13**	.21**	.22**	.24**	.43**	1		
EWB	.15**	.07	.34**	.12**	.27**	.12**	.26**	.15**	.34**	.31**	-.09*	.26**	.03	.25**	-.00	.26**	.17**	.24**	.27**	.29**	.39**	.60**	1	
HF	.19**	.11**	.34**	.14**	.30**	.13**	.29**	.17**	.37**	.34**	-.09*	.29**	.02	.26**	.02	.29**	.17**	.25**	.28**	.30**	.44**	.78**	.97**	1

Note 1: YOM = Years of Marriage, KIN = Kindness, IND = Indifference, CoH = Common Humanity, SEP = Separation, MIN = Mindfulness, DIS = Disengagement, CFO = Compassion for Others, SK = Self-Kindness, SJ = Self-Judgment, CH = Common Humanity, I = Isolation, M = Mindfulness, OI = Over-Identification, SCS = Self-Compassion Scale, FS = Forgiveness of self, FO = Forgiveness of others, FOS = Forgiveness of situation, HFS = Heartland Forgiveness Scale, IDH = Interdependent Happiness, HWB = Hedonic Well-being, EWB = Eudaimonic Well-being and HF = Human Flourishing

Note 2: *. Correlation is significant at the .05 level, **. Correlation is significant at the .01 level

Disengagement showed significant positive correlations with hedonic well-being ($r = .18$, $p = .01$), eudaimonic well-being ($r = .15$, $p = .01$) and human flourishing ($r = .17$, $p = .01$) of all the participants. Overall compassion for others showed significant positive correlations with interdependent happiness ($r = .23$, $p = .01$), hedonic well-being ($r = .34$, $p = .01$), eudaimonic well-being ($r = .34$, $p = .01$) and human flourishing ($r = .37$, $p = .01$) of all the participants (see Table 4.4).

Self-kindness showed significant positive correlations with interdependent happiness ($r = .30$, $p = .01$), hedonic well-being ($r = .31$, $p = .01$), eudaimonic well-being ($r = .31$, $p = .01$) and human flourishing ($r = .34$, $p = .01$) of all the participants. Self-kindness showed significant negative correlations with the scores of self-judgement ($r = .10$, $p = .05$), isolation ($r = .17$, $p = .01$) and over-identification ($r = .09$, $p = .05$) of all the participants. Self-judgement showed significant positive correlations with interdependent happiness ($r = .13$, $p = .01$), eudaimonic well-being ($r = .09$, $p = .01$) and human flourishing ($r = .09$, $p = .01$) of all the participants (see Table 4.4).

Common humanity showed significant positive correlations with interdependent happiness ($r = .34$, $p = .01$), hedonic well-being ($r = .28$, $p = .01$), eudaimonic well-being ($r = .26$, $p = .01$) and human flourishing ($r = .29$, $p = .01$) of all the participants. Common humanity showed significant negative correlations with the scores of self-judgement ($r = .16$, $p = .01$) and over-identification ($r = .106$, $p = .01$) of all the participants (see Table 4.4).

Isolation showed significant negative correlation with interdependent happiness ($r = .14$, $p = .01$) of all the participants. Mindfulness showed significant positive correlations with interdependent happiness ($r = .28$, $p = .01$), hedonic well-being ($r = .21$, $p = .01$), eudaimonic well-being ($r = .25$, $p = .01$) and human flourishing ($r = .26$, $p = .01$) of all the participants. Mindfulness showed significant negative correlations only with the scores of self-judgement ($r = .10$, $p = .01$) of all the participants (see Table 4.4).

Overall self-compassion showed significant positive correlations with interdependent happiness ($r = .22$, $p = .01$), hedonic well-being ($r = .28$, $p = .01$), eudaimonic well-being ($r = .26$, $p = .01$) and human flourishing ($r = .29$, $p = .01$) of all the participants. Forgiveness of self showed significant positive correlations with interdependent happiness ($r = .13$, $p = .01$), hedonic well-being ($r = .13$, $p = .01$), eudaimonic well-being ($r = .17$, $p = .01$) and human flourishing ($r = .17$, $p = .01$) of all the participants. Forgiveness of others showed significant positive correlations with interdependent happiness ($r = .12$, $p = .01$), hedonic well-being ($r = .21$, $p = .01$), eudaimonic well-being ($r = .24$, $p = .01$) and human flourishing ($r = .35$, $p = .01$) of all the participants (see Table 4.4).

Forgiveness of situation showed significant positive correlations with interdependent happiness ($r = .15$, $p = .01$), hedonic well-being ($r = .22$, $p = .01$), eudaimonic well-being ($r = .27$, $p = .01$) and human flourishing ($r = .28$, $p = .01$) of all the participants. Overall forgiveness showed significant positive correlations with interdependent happiness ($r = .17$, $p = .01$), hedonic well-being ($r = .24$, $p = .01$), eudaimonic well-being ($r = .29$, $p = .01$) and human flourishing ($r = .30$, $p = .01$) of all the participants (see Table 4.4).

4.2 SECTION TWO: HIERARCHICAL REGRESSION ANALYSIS

4.2.1 Hierarchical Regression Analysis for Interdependent Happiness

In Table 4.5 The demographic variables (education, gender, age, years of marriage and nature of family) were entered at step 1, kindness, indifference, common humanity, separation, mindfulness, and disengagement were entered at step 2, self-kindness, self-judgement, common humanity, isolation, mindfulness, and over-identification were entered at step 3, the forgiveness of self, forgiveness of others, and forgiveness of situation were entered at step 4 in a stepwise fashion (see Table 4.5). It is explicit in Table 4.5 that the demographic variables (education, gender, age, years of marriage and nature of family) accounted for a significant variance by contributing 2.90% in the scores of interdependent happiness in model 1 (R^2 = .029, $F(5, 594)$ = 3.60, p = .003).

The results show that the predicted value of interdependent happiness for the joint family is .109 units higher than for the nuclear family in model 1. The addition, compassion for others (kindness, indifference, common humanity, separation, mindfulness, and disengagement) at step 2 accounted for 14.30% variance in interdependent happiness (R^2 = .143, $F(6, 588)$ = 12.97, p = .000). The predicted value of interdependent happiness increases significantly by .112, .164, and .158 units for each unit of kindness, common humanity, and mindfulness component of compassion for others, respectively. Addition of the component of self-compassion (self-kindness, self-judgement, common humanity, isolation, mindfulness, and over-identification) at step 3 shows that the predicted values of interdependent happiness increase .121, .180 and .095 units for each unit of SK, CH, OI, respectively whereas decreases .096 unit for each unit of over-identification. Overall, self-compassion contributes 21.80% variability in interdependent happiness (R^2 = .218, $F(6, 582)$ = 9.326, p = .000). Forgiveness measures did not contribute significant variance in interdependent happiness as stated in Model 4 (R^2 = .222, $F(3, 579)$ = 0.93, p = .428).

Table 4.5

Hierarchical Regression Analysis: Biographic Details, Compassion for Others, Self-Compassion and Forgiveness for Interdependent Happiness

Predictors	Model 1					Model 2					Model 3					Model 4				
	B	SE	β	t	p	B	SE	β	t	p	B	SE	β	t	p	B	SE	β	t	p
Education	-.57	.60	-.04	-.95	.34	.05	.58	.00	.09	.93	.16	.56	.01	.28	.78	.21	.57	.02	.37	.71
Gender	-.31	.57	-.02	-.54	.59	-.43	.54	-.03	-.80	.43	.05	.53	.00	.10	.92	.05	.53	.00	.10	.92
Age	.06	.07	.07	.86	.39	-.01	.06	-.02	-.23	.82	-.03	.06	-.04	-.52	.61	-.03	.06	-.04	-.57	.57
YOM	.04	.06	.05	.60	.55	.06	.06	.08	1.05	.30	.07	.06	.08	1.13	.26	.08	.06	.09	1.26	.21
NOF	-1.50	.56	-.11	-2.66	.01	-1.46	.54	-.11	-2.73	.01	-1.38	.52	-.10	-2.66	.01	-1.33	.52	-.10	-2.55	.01
KIN						.23	.10	.11	2.35	.02	.07	.10	.04	.76	.45	.07	.10	.03	.69	.49
IND						-.01	.10	-.01	-.09	.93	-.01	.10	-.01	-.10	.92	-.01	.10	-.01	-.10	.92
CoH						.381	.10	.16	3.69	.00	.28	.10	.12	2.69	.01	.28	.11	.12	2.68	.01
SEP						-.16	.10	-.07	-1.43	.15	-.14	.11	-.06	-1.30	.19	-.14	.11	-.06	-1.31	.19
MIN						.36	.10	.16	3.50	.00	.27	.10	.12	2.54	.01	.26	.11	.11	2.48	.01
DIS						.01	.11	.00	.05	.96	-.08	.10	-.04	-.78	.44	-.07	.11	-.04	-.68	.50
SK											.21	.08	.12	2.77	.01	.21	.08	.12	2.81	.01
SJ											-.07	.07	-.04	-.98	.33	-.07	.07	-.04	-.96	.34
CH											.33	.08	.18	3.92	.00	.32	.08	.18	3.87	.00
I											-.18	.08	-.10	-2.19	.03	-.18	.08	-.10	-2.21	.03
M											.11	.09	.06	1.30	.20	.10	.09	.06	1.16	.25
OI											.18	.08	.10	2.15	.03	.17	.08	.09	2.00	.05
FS																.10	.06	.06	1.48	.14
FO																-.05	.06	-.04	-.88	.38
FOS																.03	.07	.02	.36	.72
R^2	.029					.143					.218					.222				
ΔR^2	.029					.113					.075					.004				
ΔF	3.60**					12.97**					9.33**					0.93				

Note 1. YOM = Years of Marriage, NOF = Nature of Family, KIN = Kindness, IND = Indifference, CoH = Common Humanity, SEP = Separation, MIN = Mindfulness, DIS = Disengagement, SK = Self-Kindness, SJ = Self-Judgment, CH = Common Humanity, I = Isolation, M = Mindfulness, OI = Over-Identification, FS = Forgiveness of self, FO = Forgiveness of others, FOS = Forgiveness of situation, and IDH = Interdependent Happiness.

Note 2. *. Correlation is significant at the 0.05 level, **. Correlation is significant at the 0.01 level.

Note 3. N = 600

4.2.2 Hierarchical Regression Analysis for Hedonic Well-Being

In Table 4.6, the demographic variables (education, gender, age, years of marriage and nature of family) were entered at step 1, kindness, indifference, common humanity, separation, mindfulness, and disengagement were entered at step 2, self-kindness, self-judgement, common humanity, isolation, mindfulness, and over-identification were entered at step 3, the forgiveness of self, forgiveness of others, and forgiveness of situation were entered at step 4 in a stepwise fashion (see Table 4.6). Table 4.6 shows that the predicted value of hedonic well-being for graduate is .090 units higher than for the non-graduate in model 1 (R^2 = .066, $F(5, 594)$ = 8.410, p = .000). The addition of compassion for others accounted for 16.50% variance in hedonic well-being (R^2 =.165, $F(6, 588)$ = 11.67, p = .000).

The predicted value of hedonic well-being increases significantly by .162 and .163 units for each unit of common humanity and mindfulness components of compassion for others, respectively. Addition of self-compassion at step 3 shows that the predicted values of hedonic well-being increases .202, .107 and .110 units for each unit of self-kindness, common humanity, over-identification, respectively whereas decreases .090 units for each units of self judgement (R^2 = .165, $F(6, 588)$ 11.67, p = .000). Overall, self compassion contribute 22.30% variability to hedonic well-being (R^2 =.223, $F(6, 582)$ = 7.19, p = .000). Forgiveness measures did not contribute significant variance to hedonic well-being in depicted in Model 4 (R^2 = .227, $F(3, 579)$ = 0.90, p = .442).

Table 4.6

Hierarchical Regression Analysis: Biographic Details, Compassion for Others, Self-Compassion and Forgiveness for Hedonic Well-being

Predictors	Model 1					Model 2					Model 3					Model 4				
	B	SE	β	t	p	B	SE	β	t	p	B	SE	β	t	p	B	SE	β	t	p
Education	-.75	.34	-.09	-2.19	.03	-.23	.33	-.03	-.71	.48	-.24	.32	-.03	-.74	.46	-.20	.32	-.02	-.61	.54
Gender	-.44	.32	-.06	-1.38	.17	-.51	.31	-.07	-1.66	.10	-.42	.30	-.06	-1.38	.17	-.43	.30	-.06	-1.41	.16
Age	.06	.04	.13	1.69	.09	.03	.04	.05	.72	.47	.01	.03	.03	.37	.71	.01	.04	.03	.35	.73
YOM	.04	.04	.09	1.16	.25	.04	.04	.08	1.16	.25	.05	.03	.10	1.49	.14	.05	.03	.10	1.48	.14
NOF	-.58	.32	-.07	-1.82	.07	-.62	.30	-.08	-2.03	.04	-.66	.30	-.08	-2.23	.03	-.63	.30	-.08	-2.10	.04
KIN						.05	.06	.04	.91	.37	-.01	.06	-.01	-.15	.89	-.02	.06	-.01	-.29	.78
IND						.01	.06	.01	.22	.83	.02	.06	.02	.37	.71	.02	.06	.02	.38	.71
CoH						.22	.06	.16	3.71	.00	.20	.06	.15	3.36	.00	.19	.06	.14	3.11	.00
SEP						.09	.06	.07	1.39	.17	.07	.06	.05	1.09	.28	.07	.06	.05	1.10	.27
MIN						.22	.06	.16	3.65	.00	.19	.06	.15	3.21	.00	.18	.06	.14	3.04	.00
DIS						.06	.06	.05	.96	.34	.01	.06	.01	.24	.81	.01	.06	.01	.13	.90
SK											.20	.04	.20	4.65	.00	.192	.04	.20	4.44	.00
SJ											-.09	.04	-.09	-2.15	.03	-.10	.04	-.10	-2.30	.02
CH											.11	.05	.11	2.34	.02	.11	.05	.11	2.28	.02
I											.06	.05	.05	1.21	.23	.05	.05	.05	1.10	.27
M											-.08	.05	-.08	-1.63	.10	-.09	.05	-.09	-1.79	.07
OI											.12	.05	.11	2.51	.01	.11	.05	.10	2.21	.03
FS																.04	.04	.04	1.04	.30
FO																.01	.03	.01	.17	.86
FOS																.04	.04	.04	.91	.36
R^2	.066					.165					.223					.227				
ΔR^2	.066					.099					.058					.004				
ΔF	8.41**					11.67**					7.19**					0.90				

Note 1. YOM = Years of Marriage, NOF = Nature of Family, KIN = Kindness, IND = Indifference, CoH = Common Humanity, SEP = Separation, MIN = Mindfulness, DIS = Disengagement, SK = Self-Kindness, SJ = Self-Judgment, CH = Common Humanity, I = Isolation, M = Mindfulness, OI = Over-Identification, FS = Forgiveness of self, FO = Forgiveness of others, FOS = Forgiveness of situation, and IDH = Interdependent Happiness.

Note 2. *. Correlation is significant at the 0.05 level, **. Correlation is significant at the 0.01 level.

Note 3. N = 600

4.2.3 Hierarchical Regression Analysis for Eudaimonic Well-Being

Table 4.7 shows that the predicted value of eudaimonic well-being for graduate is .198 units higher than for the non-graduate in model 1(R^2 = .090, F(5, 594) = 11.72, p = .000). The predicted value of eudaimonic well-being for the joint family is .114 units higher than for the nuclear family in model 1. Similarly, the predicted value of eudaimonic well-being increases significantly by .241 units for age. The addition of compassion for others accounted 19.50% variance in eudaimonic well-being (R^2 = .195, F(6, 588) = 12.77, p = .000).

The predicted value of eudaimonic well-being increases significantly by .212 and .099 units for each unit of kindness and common humanity component of compassion for others, respectively. Addition of self-compassion at step 3 shows that the predicted value of eudaimonic well-being increases .192 and .098 units for each unit of self-kindness and I whereas decreases .085 units for each unit of self-judgment. Overall, self-compassion contributes 23.80% in the variability of eudaimonic well-being (R^2 = .238, F(6, 582) = 5.53, p = .000). The addition of the various components of forgiveness measure at step 4 shows that the predicted values of eudaimonic well-being increase .096 units for each unit of forgiveness of situation. Overall, forgiveness contributes 25.30% in the variability of eudaimonic well-being as depicted in Model 4 (R^2 = .253, F(3, 579) 3.85, p = .010).

Table 4.7

Hierarchical Regression Analysis: Biographic Details, Compassion for Others, Self-Compassion and Forgiveness for Eudaimonic Well-Being

Predictors	Model 1					Model 2					Model 3					Model 4				
	B	SE	β	t	p	B	SE	β	t	p	B	SE	β	t	p	B	SE	β	t	p
Education	-4.25	.87	-.20	-4.89	.00	-2.98	.84	-.14	-3.55	.00	-3.02	.83	-.14	-3.65	.00	-2.83	.83	-.13	-3.43	.00
Gender	.51	.82	.07	.62	.54	.34	.78	.02	.44	.66	.51	.78	.03	.66	.51	.43	.77	.02	.56	.57
Age	.30	.09	.24	3.22	.00	.19	.09	.16	2.17	.03	.16	.09	.13	1.79	.07	.16	.09	.13	1.80	.07
YOM	-.15	.09	-.12	-1.58	.12	-.14	.09	-.11	-1.53	.13	-.10	.09	-.08	-1.15	.25	-.11	.09	-.09	-1.30	.20
NOF	-2.33	.81	-.11	-2.87	.00	-2.56	.77	-.13	-3.31	.00	-2.55	.77	-.12	-3.33	.00	-2.39	.76	-.12	-3.14	.00
KIN						.65	.14	.21	4.60	.00	.53	.14	.17	3.74	.00	.49	.14	.16	3.45	.00
IND						.03	.15	.01	.20	.84	.04	.15	.01	.27	.79	.04	.15	.01	.29	.77
CoH						.35	.15	.09	2.31	.02	.28	.15	.08	1.83	.07	.19	.15	.05	1.22	.23
SEP						.20	.16	.06	1.28	.20	.17	.16	.05	1.10	.27	.18	.16	.05	1.16	.25
MIN						.27	.15	.08	1.80	.07	.16	.15	.05	1.07	.29	.11	.15	.03	.71	.48
DIS						.04	.15	.02	.28	.78	-.03	.15	-.01	-.19	.85	-.09	.15	-.03	-.61	.54
SK											.49	.11	.19	4.45	.00	.44	.11	.17	3.94	.00
SJ											-.22	.11	-.09	-2.05	.04	-.27	.11	-.11	-2.54	.01
CH											.13	.12	.05	1.03	.30	.12	.12	.04	.98	.33
I											.27	.12	.10	2.26	.02	.24	.12	.09	2.01	.05
M											-.05	.13	-.02	-.39	.69	-.10	.13	-.04	-.74	.46
OI											.06	.12	.02	.47	.64	-.01	.12	-.01	-.11	.91
FS																.08	.09	.03	.88	.38
FO																.12	.08	.07	1.48	.14
FOS																.23	.10	.10	2.20	.03
R^2	.090					.195					.238					.253				
ΔR^2	.090					.105					.043					.015				
ΔF	11.72**					12.77**					5.53**					3.85**				

Note 1. YOM = Years of Marriage, NOF = Nature of Family, KIN = Kindness, IND = Indifference, CoH = Common Humanity, SEP = Separation, MIN = Mindfulness, DIS = Disengagement, SK = Self-Kindness, SJ = Self-Judgment, CH = Common Humanity, I = Isolation, M = Mindfulness, OI = Over-Identification, FS = Forgiveness of self, FO = Forgiveness of others, FOS = Forgiveness of situation, and IDH = Interdependent Happiness.

Note 2. *. Correlation is significant at the 0.05 level, **. Correlation is significant at the 0.01 level.

Note 3. N = 600

4.2.4 Hierarchical Regression Analysis for Human Flourishing (Well-being)

Table 4.8 shows that the predicted value of human flourishing for graduate is .183 units higher than for the non-graduate in model 1 (R^2 = .090, $F(5, 594)$ = 11.76, p = .000). The predicted value of human flourishing for the joint family is .112 units higher than for the nuclear family in model 1. The predicted value of human flourishing increases significantly by .229 units for age. The addition, measures of compassion for others accounted for 20.80% variance in human flourishing (R^2 = .208, $F(6, 588)$ = 14.64, p = .000).

The predicted value of human flourishing increases significantly by .180, .128 and .112 units for each unit of kindness, common humanity and mindfulness component of compassion for others, respectively. Addition, various component self-compassion at step 3 shows that the predicted values of human flourishing increase .213 and .093 units for each unit of self-kindness and isolation, respectively whereas decreases .094 unit for each unit of self-judgment. Overall, self-compassion contributes 26.30% in the variability of human flourishing in model 3 (R^2 = .263, $F(6, 582)$ = 7.136, p = .000). In addition, entering the three components of forgiveness measure at step 4 shows that the predicted value of human flourishing increases .088 units for each unit of forgiveness of situation in model 4. Overall, forgiveness contributes 27.50% in the variability of human flourishing as stated in Model 4 (R^2 =.275, $F(3, 579)$ = 3.38, p = .018).

Table 4.8

Hierarchical Regression Analysis: Biographic Details, Compassion for Others, Self-Compassion and Forgiveness for Human Flourishing

Predictors	Model 1					Model 2					Model 3					Model 4				
	B	SE	β	t	p	B	SE	β	t	p	B	SE	β	t	p	B	SE	β	t	p
Education	-4.10	1.10	-.18	-4.53	.00	-3.21	1.06	-.12	-3.04	.00	-3.25	1.03	-.11	-3.15	.00	-3.03	1.03	-.11	-2.93	.00
Gender	.06	1.05	.00	.06	.95	-.17	.99	-.01	-.17	.86	.10	.97	.00	.10	.92	.01	.97	.00	.01	.10
Age	.36	.12	.23	3.06	.00	.22	.11	.14	1.94	.05	.17	.11	.11	1.55	.12	.17	.11	.11	1.55	.12
YOM	-.10	.12	-.07	-.88	.38	-.10	.11	-.06	-.86	.39	-.05	.11	-.03	-.46	.65	-.06	.11	-.04	-.57	.57
NOF	-2.90	1.03	-.11	-2.82	.01	-3.18	.97	-.12	-3.26	.00	-3.21	.96	-.12	-3.36	.00	-3.02	.95	-.12	-3.17	.00
KIN						.70	.18	.18	3.94	.00	.52	.18	.13	2.95	.00	.47	.18	.12	2.67	.01
IND						.04	.19	.01	.23	.82	.06	.19	.02	.33	.74	.07	.19	.02	.35	.72
CoH						.56	.19	.13	2.99	.00	.47	.19	.11	2.51	.01	.37	.19	.08	1.95	.05
SEP						.29	.20	.07	1.45	.15	.24	.20	.06	1.22	.22	.25	.19	.06	1.27	.20
MIN						.49	.19	.11	2.57	.01	.36	.19	.08	1.86	.06	.29	.19	.07	1.52	.13
DIS						.10	.19	.03	.52	.60	-.02	.19	-.00	-.08	.94	-.09	.19	-.02	-.45	.65
SK											.69	.14	.21	5.01	.00	.63	.14	.19	4.54	.00
SJ											-.31	.13	-.09	-2.31	.02	-.37	.13	-.11	-2.75	.01
CH											.24	.15	.07	1.56	.12	.23	.15	.07	1.50	.14
I											.33	.15	.09	2.18	.03	.29	.15	.08	1.95	.05
M											-.13	.16	-.04	-.82	.41	-.19	.16	-.05	-1.16	.25
OI											.18	.15	.05	1.16	.25	.09	.15	.03	.61	.54
FS																.12	.12	.04	1.03	.30
FO																.12	.10	.05	1.23	.22
FOS																.27	.13	.09	2.05	.04
R^2	.090					.208					.263					.275				
ΔR^2	.090					.118					.054					.013				
ΔF	11.76**					14.64**					7.13**					3.38*				

Note 1. YOM = Years of Marriage, NOF = Nature of Family, KIN = Kindness, IND = Indifference, CoH = Common Humanity, SEP = Separation, MIN = Mindfulness, DIS = Disengagement, SK = Self-Kindness, SJ = Self-Judgment, CH = Common Humanity, I = Isolation, M = Mindfulness, OI = Over-Identification, FS = Forgiveness of self, FO = Forgiveness of others, FOS = Forgiveness of situation, and IDH = Interdependent Happiness.

Note 2. *. Correlation is significant at the 0.05 level, **. Correlation is significant at the 0.01 level.

Note 3. N = 600

CHAPTER – 5

DISCUSSION

DISCUSSION

The findings of the study proved the contention that intrapersonal and interpersonal resources (compassion for others, self-compassion and forgiveness) carry significant role in shaping the nature and extent of well-being and interdependent happiness of the Hindu married couples. The findings of the study exhibited that demographic attributes (age and years of marriage), compassion for others, self-compassion and forgiveness showed significant relationships with the interdependent happiness and well-being of the Hindu married couples. It was evident that demographic factors (education, gender, age, years of marriage and nature of family), compassion for others and self-compassion accounted for significant variance in the scores of interdependent happiness of the married couples. These findings provide partial support for the study hypotheses.

5.1 Demographic Factors, Interdependent Happiness and Well-Being

The findings showed that the greater the age of the participants the higher was their interdependent happiness. It may be because over time, people develop better control over their behaviours and emotions and develop a better understanding of the realities of life events. A study has argued that as people grow older, they become more self-compassionate which, in turn, may buffer against the negative life outcomes on one hand and enhance positive outcomes on the other (Brown et al., 2019). According to Erikson and Erikson (1997), intimacy, generativity and ego-integrity increase as people get older which make them inclined to cultivate love, care and wisdom. These additions facilitate a better understanding of self, others and realities of life which, in turn, make people happier. Indian society extends more privilege and respect to older people which may be another cause of increasing interdependent happiness of the couples. The participants of the current study may have achieved children, employment and social recognition with their increasing age, which may be another reason for a positive correlation between their age and interdependent happiness.

The finding showed that gender did not contribute significant variability in the scores of interdependent happiness of the couples. Conversely, previous studies have shown that there are significant gender differences in emotional and social skills of men and women. For instance, women experience higher positive emotions than men. They are also better at regulating their emotions and more skilled at managing their interpersonal relations (Hitokoto & Uchida, 2015). Studies have also shown that men possess higher self-acceptance and autonomy than women while women show higher scores on personal growth and positive relations with others than men (Gómez-Baya et al., 2018; Matud et al., 2019). The happiness of women is more guided by positive relationships, care and interdependence than men (Moriyama et al., 2018). Women also show the higher ability of emotion recognition, social sensitivity, close friendships, empathy and differential use of the areas of the brain (Moriyama et al., 2018; Wong et al., 2020). The equal opportunities in education, social interaction and exposure, employment and other avenues may have reduced differences in social and emotional skills of the male and female participants of the current study. These avenues may have also reduced the gap between their self-acceptance, feeling of autonomy and positive relationships as stated in some previous studies. These might be the possible reasons behind no gender difference in the interdependent happiness measure of the current study.

The findings of the current study showed that the joint family had a positive role in shaping the interdependent happiness of the couples. It has been suggested that the joint family helps in preserving and protecting interdependence in relationships, mutuality, cooperation and positive regards to significant others. These attributes of the joint family may have a direct role in shaping the interdependent happiness of the couples. Moreover, the joint family plays an important role in preserving meaning, relationship, positive living and positive values (Krys et al., 2019). A joint family cultivates a strong adherence to religious and spiritual practices than a nuclear family (Gautam, 2020; Tiwari, Singh, et al., 2020). Taken together, these strengths of a joint family may be argued to enhance self-understanding, realities of life, resourcefulness, quality of life and relational positive outcomes which might be the possible reasons behind its positive contribution in the interdependent happiness of the married Hindu couples. Joint or nuclear families may also differ in their interpersonal engagements, positive communication and investment of time in relationships which, in turn, may explain their differential relationship with interdependent happiness.

The age, years of marriage (length of married life) and the three facets of forgiveness showed positive correlations with all the three dimensions of well-being. Age emerged as the most significant factors to account for significant change in hedonic and psychological well-being, respectively. Conversely, the forgiveness of others did the same eudaimonic well-being and human flourishing. Various biographic attributes exhibited dissimilar predictive strengths to different indices of well-being in Model 1. For example, education, gender and age exhibited their positive significant predictive potentials for social, psychological and eudaimonic well-being and overall well-being. Similarly, the length of married life negatively shaped social and eudaimonic well-being. The nature of family (nuclear or joint) negatively predicted psychological well-being of married Hindu couples.

Education, gender and age exhibited significant predictive potentials for social, psychological and eudaimonic well-being and flourishing. The findings showed the role of biographic factors and self-resources in regulating the well-being of couples. A multitude of worldly life and spiritual goals have been appended with Hindu marriage. With the increasing influence of postmodern lifestyle, the demographic factors (age, joint family, years of marriage) have become important in the lives of couples. The findings of the study demonstrated that demographic factors, compassion for others, self-compassion and forgiveness significantly shaped the nature and extent of the various dimensions of the well-being of married Hindu couples. It was evident that some demographic factors (education, age, domicile, occupation and length of marriage) and self-kindness, common humanity and mindfulness (positive dimensions of self-compassion) were positively correlated with the well-being measures of the couples. On the other hand, self-judgement, isolation and over-identification (negative dimensions of self-compassion) showed either low positive or negative correlations with these measures. The regression analyses showed that some biographic factor (education, gender, age, length of the marriage and nature of family) accounted for significant variability in the scores of the various aspects of well-being in a dissimilar manner. Self-kindness and common humanity introduced positive variability while self-judgement caused negative variability in the various indices of well-being.

It was evident that education, gender and age accounted for positive variability in the various indices of the well-being of the couples. It may be argued that higher level of educational attainments has been reported to be directly associated with the understanding, knowledge, better employment opportunities, attributions, ability to face adversities and become resilient towards the happenings of life (Darling-Hammond et al., 2019; Osher et al., 2014; Sylva, 1994). This might be the reason behind its positive contribution to the well-being measures. Moreover, the males (husbands) have shown better performance on the various measures of well-being as compared to their females (wives). It has been argued that Indian society still carries large and perceptible gender disparities in the availability of various resources and opportunities (Ram et al., 2014). It has been argued that gender differences in well-being in favour of the males may occur as a result of differential availabilities of the socio-cultural and socialization patterns along with positive self-resources like self-forgiveness, self-compassion and self-esteem (Pandey et al., 2019a, 2019b). Over time in married life, both husbands and wives become familiar and adapt to the various realities of life. This might be the reason behind positive contributions of the greater length of married life on the well-being measures (Diener et al., 2000; Perkins et al., 2016). Nature of Family (nuclear or joint) also is argued to prompt differential kinds of experiences, resources and opportunities that may be closely associated with the experiences of well-being. This discussion makes it apparent that demographic factors are very important in ascertaining the nature and extent of the well-being of married Hindu couples for various genuine reasons.

Education provides individuals with an opportunity to widen their cognitive, affective and behavioural horizons and enhances the feeling of self-worth, efficacy, self-esteem and general understanding. These attributes of education might be behind its positive correlations and predictive strengths for social and psychological well-being. Indian society is still known for its traditional practices and cultural values. Here in Indian society, being male makes assured availability of social and psychological resources. For example, men are still assumed as more skilled, entrepreneur, worthy, and suitable for most of the jobs. These differential conceptualizations of gender in Indian society may have their dissimilar experiences of eudaimonic well-being.

Length of married life and the nature of family (nuclear or joint) had shown negative roles in social and psychological well-being. This may because middle adulthood is generally characterized by the demands from all sides of life, increased health issues of self and parents, the stress in work life, promotion etc. These factors may have acted as obstacles before the well-being of the participants. These factors may hinder social contribution, social coherence, social interest, positive relations with others, personal growth, autonomy and purpose in life as conceptualized in mental health continuum measure (Keyes, 2005; Lupano Perugini et al., 2017; Pandey et al., 2020).

5.2 Compassion and Interdependent Happiness

The findings clearly showed that compassion for others and self-compassion had significant correlations with and positively predicted the interdependent happiness of the participants. Similar findings have been reported by some recent studies (Muris et al., 2016, 2018; Muris & Petrocchi, 2017; Pandey et al., 2019). Self-compassion is characterized by a higher self-care, self-tolerance, self-acceptance, common struggle, a proper understanding of negative traits, appropriate perception of lack of available resources, emotional stability, stable perception, universal human inadequacy, rational thinking about failures of human life and open-mindedness to deal with painful experiences of human life (Neff, 2003b; Pandey et al., 2020). Interdependent happiness is characterized by positive evaluations, positive interpersonal role, stability in life, security, socially desirable behaviours, positive social comparison and equity (Hitokoto & Uchida, 2015). These strengths of self-compassion align with the core features of interdependent happiness, which may explain the positive relationship between self-compassion and interdependent happiness.

Compassion for others and self-compassion may also facilitate interdependent happiness as it may help individuals to make their higher presence and remain attentive to others in interpersonal contexts in place of distracted inward in being self-critical. These attributes of compassion have been suggested to help individuals to show more social connectedness and interpersonal competence (Bloch, 2018). Self-compassion has also been argued to show a close relationship with attachment (Mackintosh et al., 2018). This may be another reason behind its association with interdependent happiness. Self-compassion has been observed to motivate others to correct their interpersonal mistakes (Baker & McNulty, 2011). Self-compassion has also been reported to be linked with a greater likelihood to compromise, greater authenticity, lower levels of emotional turmoil and higher levels of relational well-being and thus, extend helping hands in resolving interpersonal conflicts (Yarnell & Neff, 2013). Other interpersonal benefits of self-compassion promotes positive affects, compassionate goals, forgiveness, self-esteem, belongingness and decreased loneliness (Liu, 2017). This increased social connectedness, interpersonal interactions with others, engagement in more self-disclosure, expression of the emotional support to others and interpersonal competence cultivated by self-compassion may be responsible for increased interdependent happiness of the couples in the present study.

Some other studies have suggested a variety of mechanisms behind the catalyzing influence of compassion for others and self-compassion on the various positive life outcomes. For example, self-compassion has been suggested to promote resilience and community orientation (Akin & Akin, 2015; Tanaka et al., 2011), thriving positive emotions, socially desirable behaviours, acceptance and useful attributions (Barnard & Curry, 2011). Self-compassionate people use 'we' more frequently in place of 'I' and exhibit higher social references to friends, family, and other persons (Neff et al., 2007), higher levels of optimism, gratitude and positive affect (Breen et al., 2010; Neff et al., 2007), emotional intelligence, wisdom, personal initiative, curiosity, intellectual flexibility, life satisfaction, and feelings of social connectedness (Heffernan et al., 2010; Martin et al., 2011; Neff et al., 2008) and feelings of autonomy, competence, relatedness and self-determination (Magnus et al., 2010). These interpersonal benefits of self-compassion may be some important reasons behind its positive association with the interdependent happiness in the present study.

5.3 Compassion and Well-Being

The study also examined the relationship among demographic factors, self-compassion and well-being among married Hindu couples. The findings showed that demographic factors (age and length of marriage) and self-kindness, common humanity and mindfulness which are assumed to reflect positive dimensions, exhibited positive relationships with well-being measures of the couples while self-judgement, isolation and over-identification did show either low positive or negative correlations with these measures. The findings exhibited that the well-being of the couples was patterned after the nature and types of self-compassion. It was evident that the positive dimensions of self-compassion showed positive correlation and significant contributions to determine the extent of the well-being of the couples.

Contrarily, self-judgement, isolation and over-identification (negative dimensions of self-compassion) showed a negative association with the various measures of well-being of the couples.

Thus, it may be argued that these protective and promotive strengths of compassion (compassion for others and self-compassion) might be the real cause behind its close link and predictive role for the various dimensions of well-being measures (Neff et al., 2007; Neff et al., 2007; Pandey et al., 2019; Pommier et al., 2019; Tiwari et al., 2019). The findings showed the role of biographic factors and self-resources in regulating the well-being of couples. A multitude of worldly and spiritual life goals have been appended with Hindu marriage. With the increasing influence of postmodern lifestyle, the socioeconomic factors have become important in the lives of couples.

In a meta-analytic review, the relationship between compassion (compassion for others and self-compassion) and well-being has been explained (Zessin et al., 2015). The review indicated the higher achievement of compassion (compassion for others and self-compassion) of female and consonant well-being as compared to the males. Moreover, females moderated a higher relationship with cognitive well-being. The geographical factors, age, education and family were reported to influence the relationship between compassion (compassion for others and self-compassion) and psychological well-being (Zessin et al., 2015). In essence, the review reported a causal relationship between compassion (compassion for others and self-compassion) and well-being. Thus, the findings of the study corroborate that compassion (compassion for others and self-compassion) plays a significant role in shaping the well-being of married Hindu couples.

5.4 Forgiveness and Interdependent Happiness

Forgiveness of self, others, situations and overall forgiveness were positively correlated with the interdependent happiness of the couples but did not predict significantly. Forgiveness of self has been suggested to enhance self-understanding, positive attributions and positive emotionality (Pandey et al., 2020; Thompson et al., 2005). Forgiveness of others catalyzes understanding of other people, interpersonal and social situations positively whereas forgiveness of situations involves realistic and positive thinking of transgressing situations and better adaptability (Thompson et al., 2005). These strengths of forgiveness fit with the conceptualization of interdependent happiness. For example, interdependent happiness, peculiar to countries like India, originates from interpersonally engaged emotions such as having friendly feelings toward others (Kitayama et al., 2006), a bond with others, social harmony, the absence of emotional disturbance, transcendental reappraisal (Yukiko Uchida & Kitayama, 2009) and interdependence goals (Oishi & Diener, 2001; Uchida & Ogihara, 2012).

These attributes of interdependent happiness may be argued to get facilitated by positive attributions, positive emotionality, a better understanding of other people, interpersonal and social situations, realistic and positive thinking of transgressing situations and better adaptability engrained by forgiveness (Thompson et al., 2005). Forgiveness may ease the achievement of interdependent goals which has been suggested to be the main precursor of interdependent happiness (Hitokoto & Uchida, 2015; Uchida et al., 2004; Uchida & Oishi, 2016). Forgiveness has been found to improve relationships (Akhtar et al., 2017; Braithwaite et al., 2011). Forgiveness helps individuals to refrain from negative cognitions and emotions and makes them more other person orientated (Maltby et al., 2005). These attributes of forgiveness may make people closer to others and develop harmonious relationships with others and thus, invest more genuine efforts to achieve interpersonal goals which are the key to interdependent happiness (Hitokoto & Takahashi, 2020).

5.5 Forgiveness and Human Flourishing (Well-being)

The role of forgiveness of self, others and situations were explicit. Self-forgiveness predicted positively social and eudaimonic well-being, and flourishing measures while others forgiveness had positive predictive value for social, psychological and eudaimonic well-being, and flourishing dimensions. Forgiveness of situations signified positive predictive strength for all the indices of well-being. It was evident that forgiveness of others carried the highest predictive strength for the eudaimonic measure while forgiveness of situations was most relevant for hedonic one. The additions of the three types of forgiveness at step 2 caused significant change ranging from 25.30% to 27.50% variability in eudaimonic well-being and flourishing measures, respectively. The predictive role of forgiveness may be understood in terms of the meaning inherent in the conceptualization of well-being in the measure.

The hedonic well-being reflected happiness, interest in life, enjoyment from various sources and satisfaction with life that may be argued to be more close to forgiveness of situations. This might have happened since forgiveness of situations reflected rational and positive thinking, perseverance, tolerance, adaptability, easy acceptance of situations and higher control of negative thoughts. Similarly, eudaimonic well-being comprised of social and psychological well-being. Social well-being signified a social contribution of an individual, integration with social realities and dynamics, actualization social goals, acceptance by others, coherence or interest in social events while psychological well-being reflected self-acceptance, environmental mastery, useful relations with others, personal growth, autonomy and purpose in life (Keyes, 2005; Lupano Perugini et al., 2017; Pandey et al., 2020). Forgiveness of self may have exerted its impacts on eudaimonic well-being as it signified self-reparation, self-criticism, self-promotion, self-acceptance and accumulation of relevant experiences. Likewise, the forgiveness of other shaped eudaimonic well-being more efficiently as it denoted non-punitive, realistic understanding of others, non-retaliation, acceptance, unconditional and positive behaviours towards others (Thompson et al., 2005).

Forgiveness of self, others and situations have shown significant positive links with all indices of well-being and slightly dissimilar predictive strengths for various well-being indices in the present study. Self-forgiveness facilitates positive self-understanding, positive frame of mind, effective attributions and positive emotionality that, in turn, may be assumed to be closely linked with social and psychological well-being. These findings have been mirrored in some earlier studies that have shown its positive links with a variety of indices of well-being (Pandey, Tiwari, Parihar, et al., 2020). Likewise, the forgiveness of others enhances positive understanding of other people, interpersonal and social situations. These strengths of forgiveness of others might be working behind its positive and predictive links with social and psychological well-being. Similar findings have also been reported by some earlier studies. Forgiveness of situations involved realistic and positive thinking of transgressing situations, better adaptability and enhanced self-understanding that might be the major reasons behind its close and predictive associations with all indices of well-being used in the present study. Indian marriage system is a sacrament that is well-structured and aims to fulfil not only worldly goals but it also acts as the means to achieve religious, social and spiritual goals of life. Through marriage one is inducted into Grahastha Ashram (householder) that helps to satisfy all worldly needs of individuals and also supports other humans and non-humans. It also helps to achieve *Dharma* (religion), *Artha* (worldly resources) and *Kama* (sensual pleasure), the three *Purusharthas* (desirable) of life. These finally lead one towards the ultimate goal of human life known as *Moksha* (salvation). This intricate nature of Hindu marriage may also complicate the associated psychological constructs like forgiveness and well-being.

5.6 Implications

The demographic factors such as education, gender, age, nature of family and length of the marriage significantly contributed to the well-being and interdependent happiness of the participants. Compassion for others, self-compassion and forgiveness evinced their significant relationships with the interdependent happiness and well-being of the couples and, thus, these intrapersonal and interpersonal resources represented significant implications for the well-being and interdependent happiness. A perusal of the findings may reflect noteworthy theory, practice and policy implications. The construct of interdependent happiness has been ascribed to collectivistic societies like India. The study observed that compassion and forgiveness are very relevant to understand positive life outcomes like well-being and interdependent happiness especially in terms of cultural attributes. The findings of the present study may be helpful to understand the dynamics essential to enhance well-being and interdependent happiness. The study lays special emphasis on the new psychological construct of interdependent happiness, hitherto little known aspect of happiness. Studying the role of demographic factors such as age, gender and nature of family (joint or nuclear in shaping well-being and interdependent happiness constitute the other strength of this study. The work also denotes cultural significance. This study will help fill the gap on the research on compassion, forgiveness, well-being and interdependent happiness which has been limited in applications with diverse populations and cultures, particularly because of the difference between individualistic and collectivistic conceptualizations of these constructs.

The findings necessitate further research to understand the prevalence of well-being and interdependent happiness constructs and their implications in diverse cultural settings. The work may facilitate basic research and professional application of positive psychological constructs. The intervention plans based on self-compassion and forgiveness may be developed to enhance social and interpersonal skills. The findings showed that some demographic factors such as age, nature of family and length of married life are relevant to understand the dynamics of compassion, forgiveness, well-being and interdependent happiness. There may be some cultural differences in these constructs. The implications of this study extend from policy and practise to theory at the individual, group, community to larger group levels. The focus should shift from individual-level factors to at least family-level factors since the nature of family seems particularly important in predicting well-being and interdependent happiness.

5.7 Limitations of the Study

Like all scientific endeavours, the current study is also marred by some limitations. For instance, the selection of the sample from a limited geographical region is one limitation. Use of a small number of psychological constructs is another limitation as the inclusion of other variables like self-construal, personality and other positive psychological constructs may have helped to come up with more insightful findings. Another limitation is the use of translated versions of the scales which may have resulted in a lower alpha value of the SCS for the current sample than suggested by the pioneers of the field (Neff, 2003b; Neff et al., 2017; Neff et al., 2019). Use of only the quantitative method constitutes another limitation.

5.8 Directions for Future Research

The scientific study of compassion, forgiveness, interdependent happiness and human flourishing (human well-being) is still in its infancy. There are many avenues for future researchers to extend their contributions to this emerging field. The constructs of compassion, forgiveness, well-being and interdependent happiness need further re-conceptualization in different cross-cultural settings to come up with its true nature and correlates. Use of qualitative methods, mixed methods and large scale studies on diverse samples may be another avenue for future researchers. New tools for measuring these constructs may be developed on diverse cultural samples. Forgiveness and self-compassion-based interventions for health and well-being need further inquiry to make it popular and practical. Future researchers may contribute further to this field by adding some more variables to understand well the nature of well-being and interdependent happiness of married couples.

CPSIA information can be obtained
at www.ICGtesting.com
Printed in the USA
LVHW081154241122
733912LV00015B/757

9 781805 450368